Student Learning Guide to Accompany

New Society
Sociology for the 21st Century

Second Edition

Robert J. Brym

Prepared by
Deborah Boutilier

HARCOURT
BRACE
CANADA

Harcourt Brace & Company, Canada
Toronto Montreal Fort Worth New York Orlando
Philadelphia San Diego London Sydney Tokyo

Canadian Cataloguing in Publication Data

Boutilier, Deborah
    Student learning guide to accompany New society : sociology for the 21st century, second edition, Robert J. Brym

ISBN 0-7747-3623-2

1. Sociology – Problems, exercises, etc. I. Brym, Robert J., 1951- . New society : sociology for the 21st century. II. Title.

HM51.B897 1998 Suppl.   301   C97-932626-5

Acquisitions Editor: Ken Nauss
New Media Co-ordinator: Kelly Nakamura
Ancillaries Co-ordinator: Tanya Mossa
Cover Design: Sonya V. Thursby/Opus House Inc.
Printing and Binding: Webcom Limited

This book was printed in Canada.

1 2 3 4 5   02 01 00 99 98

PREFACE

How can I get the most out of my Student Learning Guide?

This book is called a Student Learning Guide for a specific reason. Although it looks and acts like a study manual, unlike most study manuals it is not bulky, but rather easy to carry. It is also simplistic in form and attempts, through a variety of ways, to guide your learning. You are ultimately responsible for actually accumulating and retaining educational knowledge, however, this book will assist you in guiding your learning, so that it becomes something enjoyable, not stressful. This Student Learning Guide does not repeat a lot of what is in the textbook, but rather allows you to put that information to good use through the use of both objective and subjective exercises. Carry this with you in your knapsack and pull it out when you get a chance – in between classes, over morning coffee, or even while waiting for the bus. You'll be amazed at how much this little book can offer, but even more amazed at how much it can make you think!

True/False and Multiple Choice Questions

Objective-type questions not only test how much you remember from the textbook, they also make you think about what you've learned and what makes you remember what you've learned. From these questions, try to develop your learning skills and identify the tricks that you can use to help you retain material from the textbook. These questions are not designed simply to test your memory recall. These are tools that you can use to help you learn. Your scores here should be a good indication of how well you understand each chapter. If your scores are not good (i.e., less than 60 percent), reread your chapter and try again. These questions are especially designed to help you prepare for any upcoming objective-examinations and should act as good indicators of your potential performance levels.

Critical Thinking Questions

The study of sociology can be defined as the method by which ordinary people strive to understand what is happening to them and their society. Systematic observation of the structures, institutions, and forces in society encourage us to look beyond the strictly personal and individual events that affect our lives, allowing us to use our critical thinking skills and see the world from a different, more global perspective. The need for such understanding is urgent at this present historical moment when change is rapid. Unprecedented opportunities to build a better world and improve the quality of life for many people lie ahead. The study of sociology can help you figure out how society works and what you can do to change it by developing a sociological imagination and sociological perspective.

The critical thinking questions require you to adopt a more subjective and critical attitude to the issues at hand. While it is important to learn about sociology, it is equally important to learn how to use the skills of a sociologist. Subjective learning gives us as much of an opportunity to enrich our understanding as objective learning. When you attempt to answer these critical learning questions, actually picture yourself in the following situations, and don't be afraid to let your ideas come forth, regardless of how "off the wall" they may seem to you or to others. Critical thinking is the key to understanding all of the different facets that one idea or theory can have. Let your imagination go crazy – you'll be surprised at what you come up with!

Tips for Better Learning

1. Work on developing your reading, writing, and study skills. If your university or college offers workshops - attend them! Usually, the Student Services or Student Development centre offers classes in time management, relaxation, exam anxiety, note taking, essay writing, and study skills. These workshops are literally invaluable to your education.

2. Use your library and all of the talented people that work there. Most college and university libraries offer tours and information sessions that acquaint you with the many services they provide.

3. Get computer literate - learn how to use the Internet and the World Wide Web. This can cut your essay writing time in half. Most schools offer free two- or three-hour workshops on how to research on the Internet. I always advise my students to take a basic Computer Processing course as an elective credit in their degree. That way not only do they get the credit, they develop a very worthwhile skill.

4. Learn to type!

5. Form a study group - many students find that this is a great way to study and reinforce information that they have learned. It also allows them to interact with each other and to get to know their classmates better.

A Word to the Educators who use this Guide

Having taught a variety of sociology courses over the past seven years, I am well acquainted with the enormous amount of preparation time required to effectively present material that students will clearly understand and retain. Personally, I will take any help that I can get in that area. This Student Learning Guide has been designed to provide thought-provoking material for students, as well as teachers. The objective-type questions make great quizzes and the critical thinking questions will facilitate good group discussions and seminar presentations. I hope that you have as much fun using this book as I did in being part of its creation.

Acknowledgements

I am truly one of the lucky ones! I have been blessed with the best friends and most wonderful family in the world. I would like to thank them all for their continued love and support during my seemingly endless academic endeavours. Special thanks go out to my sister Larry, Edward "Big Guy" Luciow, the incomparable Kevin Kiss, and my Dad. Of notable mention is Mr. Don Smith, who first taught me that learning can and more importantly, should be fun. From Harcourt Brace Canada, I'd like to recognize and appreciate the efforts of Joanne Clark, Ken Nauss, and especially Kelly Nakamura. Robert J. Brym is a marvel. This one, my first, is for my Mom.

CONTENTS

TRUE OR FALSE?

(T) F   **1.**   Recent surveys of Canadian women indicate that more than half had been sexually or physically assaulted at least once in their lives, and over half were afraid to walk in their neighbourhoods at night.

T F   **2.**   Interviews with sexual assault offenders indicate that the majority suffer from psychological disorders.

T F   **3.**   According to Brym's study, a plausible explanation of the high rates of severe wife abuse in the United States where gender equality is high is "male backlash."

T F   **4.**   Research on control of modern corporations tends to support the view that control by managers and scientists is increasing.

T F   **5.**   Research indicates that work-related stress is increasing in Canada.

T F   **6.**   Brym summaries the differences between the scientific and the non-scientific approaches to knowledge with the phrase "in science, believing is seeing, whereas in everyday life, seeing is believing."

T F   **7.**   According to a 1988 study, Canadians who received B.A.s in sociology were more likely to have full-time jobs than other social science graduates.

T F   **8.**   Teenagers have the highest rates of suicide of any age category in Canada.

T F   **9.**   The primary cause of the social problems at the Grassy Narrows Indian Reserve was the pollution of the river system that prevented residents from making a living from fishing.

T F   **10.** According to Marx, the downfall of capitalist society would occur because of its inability to produce enough goods to supply the demand.

MULTIPLE CHOICE

1. In Chapter 1, Brym argues that sociology views _____ as the major causes of events happening in the world.
    (a) physical forces
    (b) social forces
    (c) psychological forces
    (d) all of the above
    (e) b and c

2. Which of the following founders of sociology was interested in both understanding Europe's transition to industrial capitalism and doing something to help make this transition better?
   (a) Marx
   (b) Durkheim
   (c) Weber
   (d) all of the above
   (e) b and c

3. According to Brym's hypothesis, the rate of severe wife abuse is higher
   (a) when men's power is higher.
   (b) when women's power is higher.
   (c) when women's power is lower.
   (d) when the ratio of men's power to women's power is higher.
   (e) when the ratio of women's power to men's power is higher.

4. Durkheim argued that suicide rates
   (a) varied directly with psychological disorders.
   (b) varied with the degree of social solidarity.
   (c) both
   (d) neither

5. All of the following are indicators of lessened social solidarity, except one. Which is the exception?
   (a) higher unemployment rates
   (b) higher divorce rates
   (c) higher religious attendance
   (d) none (i.e., all of the above are indicators)

6. C. Wright Mills argued that sociologists try to
   (a) relate individual troubles to social issues.
   (b) relate social issues to broad changes that characterize entire eras.
   (c) employ knowledge of broad social patterns to illuminate individual problems.
   (d) all of the above
   (e) a and b

7. With the development of industrial capitalism, jobs were created which typically had all of the following characteristics, except one. Which is the exception?
   (a) they required moderate to high skill levels
   (b) they involved manual labour
   (c) they were located in or near large cities
   (d) they involved long work days
   (e) none (i.e., all of the above were characteristics)

8. According to Chapter 1, workers in western Europe and North America became less interested in trying to overthrow the capitalist system because
   (a) some workers ultimately took control of industries and gained jobs in government.
   (b) workers succeeded in forcing employers to limit the length of the work day, improve work conditions, and raise wages.
   (c) workers turned their attention to fighting the introduction of technological innovation.
   (d) all of the above

9. Sociologists who have examined jobs in Canada since the 1970s have found that the fastest growing job category has been
   (a) relatively high-paying jobs.
   (b) jobs in the middle pay range.
   (c) relatively low-paying jobs.
   (d) manual and domestic jobs.
   (e) none of the above

10. According to Brym's summary, the serious flaw in the theory of postindustrialism is that
   (a) it is wrong (i.e., the evidence does not support it).
   (b) it incorrectly generalizes from changes in the top of the service sector to the whole society.
   (c) it does not take into consideration half of the population (i.e., it ignores women).
   (d) it fails to take into consideration the globalization of the economy.
   (e) none of the above

11. Approximately what proportion of employed adult Canadian women work in the "pink-collar" ghetto of sex-segregated occupations?
   (a) one-third
   (b) one-half
   (c) two-thirds
   (d) three-quarters
   (e) nine-tenths

12. In 1991, on average, women earned about _____ percent of what men earned.
   (a) 50
   (b) 60
   (c) 70
   (d) 80
   (e) 90

13. Scientific truths differ from other forms of truth in that
   (a) scientists never allow values to intrude on their observation of reality.
   (b) scientists view reality in a completely objective way.
   (c) scientific theories are systematically and publicly tested against evidence.
   (d) scientific research methods used to establish scientific truths do not yield biased results.
   (e) all of the above

14. Accepting something as true because one saw it with one's own eyes is an example of non-scientific knowledge because
   (a) it is rooted in tradition.
   (b) it is based on authority.
   (c) it is an over-generalization.
   (d) it involves premature closure of inquiry.
   (e) it is based on casual observation.

15. In 1981, the estimated dollar value of domestic work in Canada was about _____ of the gross national product.
    (a) one-third
    (b) one-half
    (c) two-thirds
    (d) three-quarters

CRITICAL THINKING

1. At the beginning of Chapter 1, Brym shares his reasons for studying sociology. Think of your reasons for taking this course. Do you have a genuine interest in learning more about this world of ours, or is this a required course for your program? Be honest with yourself and identify some concrete things that you'd like to learn more about from this course. Recognize and develop your learning objectives and, throughout the course, monitor the progress that you make toward meeting them.

2. As Weber emphasized, sociologists choose to study "only those segments of reality which have become significant to us because of their value relevance." Do you think that it is possible for a sociologist to conduct research that is completely value-free? Does the influence of a researcher's values diminish the credibility of the research? Why or why not?

3. Box 1.2 discusses capitalism and Marx's thoughts on its eventual demise. His prediction of a world with a system in which property, and therefore wealth, would be shared by everyone, has yet to see global fruition. Imagine what life would be like living in a society that banned private ownership. Would competition still exist? What would act as incentives for those positions in society that are more difficult to obtain, for example, physicians and lawyers? Could you see yourself living under these economic conditions?

4. When, in a city of 100,000 people, one person is unemployed, that is his or her personal trouble. But, when, in a nation of 50 million people, 15 million are unemployed, it becomes a public issue. Brym illustrates C. Wright Mills's notion of personal troubles and public issues by explaining the occurrence of woman abuse and suicide. Think about a situation that you can describe as being a "personal trouble." Does this trouble go beyond the personal and into the public realm? Can you better understand this individual event by looking at it on a societal level? Can you explain its existence by comparing it to similar events that occur or have occurred in society?

TRUE OR FALSE?

T   F   **1.**   According to Chapter 2 on socialization, the Rosenthal and Jacobson study shows that environmental factors are more important than biological factors in determining intelligence.

T   F   **2.**   The set of cultural norms and values used in self-evaluation and in developing concepts of the self was labelled as "society" by G.H. Mead.

T   F   **3.**   Research indicates that there is a biological factor in the cross-cultural preference of girls playing with dolls, and boys playing with toy machinery.

T   F   **4.**   Adolescence as a life stage is a product of the late nineteenth century.

T   F   **5.**   Sociologists have found that the professional socialization of medical doctors includes learning ideals about medicine's place in society.

T   F   **6.**   In Canadian society, the transition from work to retirement typically involves negative consequences.

T   F   **7.**   According to Riesman, "inner-directed" persons are typical of modern society.

T   F   **8.**   In Goffman's dramaturgical model, the self is a fragile and tentative entity.

T   F   **9.**   According to the authors of Chapter 2 on socialization, the "postmodern" condition refers to the chaos resulting from the lack of anything certain in this world.

T   F   **10.**   According to Chapter 2 on socialization, virtual sex is sometimes more satisfying than the real thing.

MULTIPLE CHOICE

1.   Which of the following statements is true?
   (a)   Structural functionalism views socialization from the point of view of the group, and symbolic interactionism views socialization from the point of view of the individual.
   (b)   Structural functionalism views socialization from the point of view of the individual, and symbolic interactionism views socialization from the point of view of the group.
   (c)   Both structural functionalism and symbolic interactionism view socialization from the point of view of the individual.
   (d)   Both structural functionalism and symbolic interactionism view socialization from the point of view of the group.
   (e)   c and d

2. Which of the following correctly states the racial hierarchy, from top to bottom, for which J. Phillipe Rushton claimed to have found evidence?
   (a) Caucasoids, Orientals, Africans
   (b) Orientals, Africans, Caucasoids
   (c) Africans, Orientals, Caucasoids
   (d) Caucasoids, Africans, Orientals
   (e) Orientals, Caucasoids, Africans

3. Which of the following are commonly found outcomes when children are raised in isolation?
   (a) early death
   (b) slow mental development
   (c) slow emotional development
   (d) all of the above
   (e) b and c

4. According to the Harlows's research with monkeys, serious, long-term consequences of prolonged isolation were due to
   (a) social isolation.
   (b) maternal deprivation.
   (c) inadequate nutrition.
   (d) lack of verbal communication.
   (e) prolonged stress.

5. In George H. Mead's scheme, the part of the personality that initiates action is called
   (a) the mind.
   (b) the self.
   (c) the me.
   (d) the I.
   (e) the generalized other.

6. According to Cooley, all of the following are major elements of the self, except one. Which is the exception?
   (a) our imagination of how we appear to others whose opinions we value
   (b) our perception of how other people judge us
   (c) a self-feeling or reaction about the judgements
   (d) our internal judgement of how consistent or inconsistent are our reactions to others
   (e) none (i.e., all of the above are major elements)

7. Parental expectations for males and females are held and communicated by parents
   (a) almost from birth.
   (b) by age one.
   (c) by age two.
   (d) by age five.
   (e) at puberty.

8. In DeLoache, Cassidy, and Carpenter's study of gender labels given to gender-neutral characters in children's books
   (a) fathers tended to assign masculine names.
   (b) mothers tended to assign masculine names.
   (c) mothers and fathers tended to assign masculine names.
   (d) mothers and fathers tended to assign feminine names.
   (e) there was no clear pattern of gender assignment to the characters.

9. Which of the following statements is true? Compared to primary socialization, adult socialization
   (a) is more compulsory.
   (b) focusses on accepting basic norms and values of the culture.
   (c) involves less control over the content and direction of socialization.
   (d) all of the above
   (e) none of the above

10. In Chapter 2 on socialization, all of the following "r" words are part of the list of "bad words" which are signposts of change in the workplace, except one. Which is the exception?
    (a) restructuring
    (b) reorganization
    (c) rationalizing
    (d) re-engineering
    (e) none (i.e., all of the above are part of the list)

11. All of the following are major contributions of the family as an agent of socialization, except one. Which is the exception?
    (a) to impart society's intellectual heritage
    (b) to teach norms, beliefs, and values
    (c) to develop the capacity for personal relationships
    (d) to form some basic attitudes
    (e) to begin the formation of a self-image

12. According to Skolnick, all of the following are macrosocial changes which strain the institution of the family, except one. Which is the exception?
    (a) an increase in "latch-key" children
    (b) decreasing age at marriage
    (c) rising divorce rates
    (d) more single-parent families
    (e) none of the above

13. According to the authors of Chapter 2 on socialization, schools teach all of the following as part of the "informal curriculum," except one. Which is the exception?
    (a) cooperation
    (b) respect for authority
    (c) creativity
    (d) conformity
    (e) discipline

14. In Goffman's dramaturgical terminology, a person who tells a white lie is engaged in
  (a) misrepresentation.
  (b) dramatic realization.
  (c) role playing.
  (d) all of the above
  (e) none of the above

15. In 1995, the top concern of Canadians was their
  (a) marital relationship.
  (b) health.
  (c) money.
  (d) job.
  (e) looks.

CRITICAL THINKING

1. The photo on page 33 automatically evokes a wide range of emotions within ourselves. How can we expect anything to survive in social isolation? Think about the people, structures, and institutions in our society that play a role in the life-long process of socialization. Do you think that we take these things for granted? If so, how? How long do you think you could last in total isolation – hours, days, months?

2. Try to think back to your grade-school days. Do you remember any of the books that your teacher used? Looking back, can you determine whether or not gender stereotyping was a part of these readers? In high school, did you feel that your teachers or guidance counsellors tried to direct you to take "gender-appropriate" classes?

3. Sociologists have debated the nature versus nurture issue for ages. Identify some of the biological and social factors that play a role in the process of socialization. In your opinion, does one set of factors play a greater role? Why or why not?

4. Brym identifies four main agents of socialization: family, peer groups, schools, and the mass media. Which of these plays the biggest role in your own socialization? Rank these four in order of importance. Do you think this order will change over time? What are some other socialization agents that play a big part in your life?

CULTURE AND THE POSTMODERN

TRUE OR FALSE?

T F   **1.** According to the chapter on culture and the postmodern, culture emerges out of the process of communication and reflection between individuals.

T F   **2.** Eating with a fork and knife in our society is a ritual.

T F   **3.** Most discourses are shared with a small segment of the population.

T F   **4.** Modern communications and the mass media have made it easier to maintain a traditional way of life.

T F   **5.** The "social construction of knowledge" refers solely to the defining of what is real by those recognized in the society as legitimate experts.

T F   **6.** According to the chapter on culture and the postmodern, those who provide knowledge generally gain power over those who learn.

T F   **7.** According to Weber, bureaucratic organizations generally employ traditional authority.

T F   **8.** The majority of Canadians feel that new immigrants to Canada should be encouraged to maintain their distinctive culture and way of life.

T F   **9.** The commodification of culture refers to the process by which symbols such as paintings are produced and sold through art galleries and art dealers, department stores, and street vendors.

T F   **10.** The ideology of multiculturalism is an example of postmodernity.

MULTIPLE CHOICE

1. The term "culture" refers to
   (a) the ideas that justify existing social arrangements.
   (b) the symbolic order through which individuals communicate.
   (c) social practices rooted in human subconsciousness.
   (d) all of the above

2. All of the following are signs, except one. Which is the exception?
   (a) the Canadian flag
   (b) a thumbs-up gesture
   (c) sacred objects
   (d) saying "see ya"
   (e) none (i.e., all of the above are signs)

3. The pervasiveness of American movies and television programs in Canadian society has been referred to by some sociologists as
   (a) cultural capitalism.
   (b) cultural imperialism.
   (c) cultural manifest destiny.
   (d) capital indoctrination.

4. Which of the following is an example of ethnocentrism?
   (a) a working-class Thunder Bay man referring to the behaviour of a white juvenile delinquent as "going Indian"
   (b) a First Nations person rejecting city life on the basis of traditional values
   (c) both
   (d) neither

5. Ideology refers to
   (a) false ideas held by a group.
   (b) the sociological study of ideas.
   (c) ideas that justify a group's interests or propose alternatives.
   (d) all of the above
   (e) none of the above

6. Ideologies which are hegemonies have all of the following properties, except one. Which is the exception?
   (a) they are "ruling ideas"
   (b) they benefit wealthy people
   (c) they benefit people who are not wealthy
   (d) people who are not wealthy accept them
   (e) none (i.e., all the above are properties)

7. In which of the following forms of music is the delegitimation of authority a common theme?
   (a) country and western
   (b) rock and roll
   (c) classical
   (d) the blues
   (e) hiphop

8. According to Pierre Bourdieu, members of the upper class possess a large amount of
   (a) cultural pluralism.
   (b) cultural capital.
   (c) popular culture.
   (d) conservative culture.
   (e) culture.

9. According to the chapter on culture and the postmodern, the working-class culture is centred around
   (a) opposition to the discipline of school.
   (b) opposition to book learning.
   (c) opposition to high culture.
   (d) opposition to bureaucracies.
   (e) drinking, driving, and fighting.

10. Parsons believed that
   (a) social change is imminent and to be feared.
   (b) social change is inhibited by rationalization.
   (c) societies are undergoing "adaptive upgrading."
   (d) societies adapt best when social change is orderly and gradual.
   (e) all of the above

11. According to Herbert Guindon, which of the following Quebec elites lost power as a result of the process of modernization which took place in Quebec over the past few decades?
   (a) the professionals
   (b) the Catholic clergy
   (c) the politicians
   (d) the landowners

12. Postmodernity is characterized by
   (a) ambiguous, chaotic, and fragmented change.
   (b) the eclectic mixing of elements from different cultures.
   (c) a fragmented sense of time.
   (d) all of the above
   (e) none of the above

13. According to A. Wilson's boxed insert in the chapter on culture and the postmodern, Canada's national parks demonstrate that
   (a) the powers of nature are greater than the powers of man.
   (b) nature in its original form is tremendously beautiful.
   (c) natural phenomena are impossible to stop.
   (d) all of the above
   (e) none of the above

14. The fact that one in five cases where an individual recalled abuse later in life also involved allegations of Satanism
   (a) provides strong support for the recording and recovery viewpoint.
   (b) provides strong support for the dispersal and construction viewpoint.
   (c) both
   (d) neither

15. The Citizen's Forum on Canada's Future identified all of the following as core Canadian values, except one. Which is the exception?
    (a) support for diversity
    (b) belief in equality of opportunity
    (c) attachment to Canada's natural beauty
    (d) belief in consultation and dialogue
    (e) none (i.e., all of the above were identified)

CRITICAL THINKING

1. Some years back, Esperanto, a universal language, was created in the hopes of increasing global communication. It was met with little enthusiasm and really never saw any great deal of success. Do you think that the possibility of a global culture is real? What social factors will influence whether or not we as individuals are willing to abandon our current culture and embrace a new one? How does the idea of the "commodification of culture" fit in here?

2. Box 3.5 discusses a list of important core values identified in Canadian culture. How closely do these values resemble your own, in terms of creating your own definition of the Canadian identity? Do you think that your values will change over time, or have they already?

3. According to a 1992 poll conducted by Maclean's, 63 percent of respondents stated that immigrants should change their culture and ways to blend with the larger society. Do you agree with this majority? Why or why not?

4. With specific reference to postmodernity, how do our increasing levels of technology impact on culture? Do you think that our culture changes as rapidly as our technology advances? What are some concrete indications that our culture is changing?

TRUE OR FALSE?

T   F   **1.**   Everyone is born either male or female.

T   F   **2.**   In almost all cultures, sex and sexuality are considered the most private and personal aspects of personal identity.

T   F   **3.**   According to the chapter on sexuality, the police pay much more attention to consensual sexual activity than to sexual abuse.

T   F   **4.**   The 1985 Ontario Law Reform Commission report on in vitro fertilization recommended that lesbians who live in a stable relationship should be able to use the services of sperm banks.

T   F   **5.**   The fundamental dividing line by which sexual identities are constructed in our culture is heterosexual versus homosexual.

T   F   **6.**   Freud's "talking cure" involves the use of the technique of "free association."

T   F   **7.**   Freud's writing consisted almost entirely of detailed descriptions of individual cases from his practice and research.

T   F   **8.**   The current Canadian Criminal Code defines obscenity as "the undue exploitation of sex."

T   F   **9.**   According to the boxed insert in the chapter on sexuality, coming out as a gay person is easier in "artsy" schools than other high schools.

T   F   **10.**   In recent surveys, the majority of Canadians say that homosexuality is "not wrong at all."

MULTIPLE CHOICE

1.   According to the chapter on sexuality, which of the following political forms accords most with human nature?
   (a)   parliamentary democracy
   (b)   direct democracy
   (c)   dictatorship
   (d)   oligarchy
   (e)   none of the above

2. According to the chapter on sexuality, the process by which we recognize, suppress, and act upon our sexuality is thoroughly
   (a) biological.
   (b) cultural.
   (c) psychological.
   (d) anthropological.
   (e) rational.

3. Male aggressiveness is turned into a norm in our society
   (a) at the level of physiological sex.
   (b) at the level of gender identity.
   (c) at the level of general cultural values.
   (d) all of the above
   (e) b and c

4. According to the text, women will be considered non-women if they excel in
   (a) risk-taking.
   (b) intelligence.
   (c) strategy.
   (d) engineering.
   (e) sports.

5. According to the chapter on sexuality, in the 1992 Butler case, the Supreme Court of Canada declared pornography to be a social evil because
   (a) it promotes sexist views of women.
   (b) sexual pictures are immoral.
   (c) both
   (d) neither

6. Presently, in our society, sex is identified with
   (a) dirt.
   (b) sin.
   (c) pleasure.
   (d) crime.
   (e) none of the above

7. Sex is often regulated by government through policies and laws concerning
   (a) population.
   (b) marriage.
   (c) the family.
   (d) all of the above
   (e) b and c

8. According to Solinger's study of maternity homes for unwed mothers in the 1950s and 1960s
   (a) black and white women were coerced into giving up their babies.
   (b) black and white women were pressured into keeping their babies.
   (c) black women were coerced into giving up their babies, but white women were pressured into keeping their babies.
   (d) white women were coerced into giving up their babies, but black women were pressured into keeping their babies.

9. According to the text, historically, Canadians ranked the races in terms of their degree of primitive, animal-like sexuality. What is this ranking, from highest to lowest degree?
   (a) black, oriental, white
   (b) black, white, oriental
   (c) oriental, black, white
   (d) oriental, white, black
   (e) white, black, oriental

10. According to the chapter on sexuality, Canada's obscenity law is problematic because
   (a) it is built on the assumption that there is a single standard of sexual morality across the nation.
   (b) it takes into account too many definitions of obscenity.
   (c) it was written by women and enforced by men.
   (d) it is not adequately enforced.

11. Which of the following studies of human sexuality were based on systematic observation?
   (a) Kinsey's
   (b) Hite's
   (c) both
   (d) neither

12. According to the text, which of the following groups goes through a long and often painful period of developing sexual identity?
   (a) homosexual males
   (b) homosexual females
   (c) heterosexual males
   (d) heterosexual females
   (e) all of the above

13. Freud compared psychoanalysis to
   (a) physics.
   (b) philosophy.
   (c) detective work.
   (d) cooking without a recipe.
   (e) cooking with a recipe.

14. According to Chodorow, conventional gender roles are reproduced as a result of
   (a) mothers' differential treatment of male and female children.
   (b) fathers' differential treatment of male and female children.
   (c) mothers' rejection of their female children.
   (d) fathers' rejection of their male children.
   (e) c and d

15. Compared to provincial human rights commissions, the federal government has responded
_____ to claims of discrimination on the basis of sexual orientation.
   (a) more favourably
   (b) equally favourably
   (c) less favourably
   (d) One cannot tell from the cases to date.

CRITICAL THINKING

1. Box 4.1 deals with the "coming out" of a young girl in high school. What are your thoughts and opinions about this? Is a person's sexual preference anybody's business but their own? How would you have reacted had this taken place in your own high school.

2. Freud's theories on sexuality are certainly thought-provoking to say the least. To what extent do you believe his explanations for our behaviour? Box 4.3 discusses his views on women's penis envy. Do these views seem valid to you? Why or why not?

3. Imagine the sheer impossibility of trying to define something as pornographic. Box 4.4 shows the courts trying to define the term "undue exploitation of sex." In this case, Butler upholds the line of cases which state that there must be one single national community standard. Do you agree with this? Is it possible to devise a single national standard? Is it fair to do so?

4. Figure 4.3 shows us that Canadians are far more tolerant of sexual pluralism than they were even ten years ago. What are some of the social factors that can account for this increasing openness? Have your own views about sexuality changed during the past five years? In which direction do you see this trend going in ten years' time? What social factors help to shape and change your opinions?

TRUE OR FALSE?

T   F   **1.**   According to the chapter on the mass media, the major effect of the media on the news is through its ability to set the news agenda.

T   F   **2.**   Since the mid-1980s, television viewing has declined slightly in Canada.

T   F   **3.**   On average, people in Canada spend more time watching television and listening to radio than working.

T   F   **4.**   According to Meyrowitz, compared to single-sense media, television allows the audience to see more of back-region behaviour.

T   F   **5.**   Orthodox Marxists emphasize the role of the media in creating hegemony.

T   F   **6.**   The consensus among researchers is that the quality of news declines when monopolization occurs in a given city or area.

T   F   **7.**   According to the text, in Quebec, Canadian-made television dramas receive stronger audience interest than does foreign programming.

T   F   **8.**   Research indicates that the trend towards technological convergence increases the privatization of everyday life.

T   F   **9.**   In general, the media view crime from the perspective of the police.

T   F   **10.**   The "sponsor effect" is likely to exaggerate the effect of violent images on aggressive behaviour among research subjects.

MULTIPLE CHOICE

1.   Which of the following categories of Canadians watches the most television?
     (a)   middle-aged housewives
     (b)   pre-adolescent and adolescent boys
     (c)   women over 60
     (d)   female children
     (e)   young adult males

2. According to the text, all of the following are major functions of the media, except one. Which is the exception?
   (a) the transmission of society's norms, values, and cultural heritage
   (b) aiding in social control
   (c) helping to integrate and maintain society as a whole
   (d) helping to provide answers to questions about the meaning of life
   (e) none (i.e., all of the above are major functions)

3. To be successful, hegemony has to incorporate
   (a) the dominant ideology.
   (b) oppositional viewpoints.
   (c) alternative viewpoints.
   (d) all of the above
   (e) a and b

4. According to the chapter on the mass media, _____ of the mass media is becoming more concentrated.
   (a) ownership
   (b) control
   (c) a and b
   (d) none of the above

5. Owning both a major league sports team and cable channel outlets which broadcast the games is an example of
   (a) vertical integration.
   (b) horizontal integration.
   (c) multi-level merger.
   (d) horizontal consolidation.
   (e) none of the above

6. Most of the revenue of daily Canadian newspapers comes from
   (a) subscription fees.
   (b) advertising.
   (c) non-newspaper revenues like investments, rents, etc.
   (d) none of the above

7. Compared to American drama, Canadian television drama is considered to be
   (a) less realistic.
   (b) more morally ambivalent.
   (c) less ironic.
   (d) all of the above
   (e) none of the above

8. Which of the following contradicts the process of representation in the media?
   (a) It involves the use of language.
   (b) It involves conscious decisions about what to include and what to leave out.
   (c) It involves unconscious decisions about what to include and what to leave out.
   (d) It involves the use of visual images and other symbolic tools.
   (e) none of the above

9. Personalization of the news is especially prevalent in
   (a) sports news coverage.
   (b) weather coverage.
   (c) political news coverage.
   (d) business news coverage.
   (e) science news coverage.

10. According to the text, all of the following categories of people are primary news sources, except one. Which is the exception?
    (a) academics
    (b) the police
    (c) corporate spokespersons
    (d) government officials
    (e) none (i.e., all of the above are primary news sources)

11. In contrast to primary news sources, secondary news sources are represented by the news media as
    (a) being analytical rather than complaining.
    (b) emphasizing what is wrong rather than offering solutions.
    (c) expressing rational ideas rather than feelings.
    (d) all of the above
    (e) none of the above

12. All of the following techniques are typically employed in Canada by the government in order to manage the media, except one. Which is the exception?
    (a) "freezing out" hostile media
    (b) giving hostile media "flak"
    (c) staging events to attract the media
    (d) sending out "trial balloons" or leaked information
    (e) none (i.e., all of the above are employed)

13. According to the chapter on the mass media, soap-opera plots revolve around the values of
    (a) the white upper class.
    (b) the suburban, alienated middle class.
    (c) the dominant corporations.
    (d) middle-class, small-town America.
    (e) left-liberal script writers.

14. The majority opinion among researchers is that television violence plays _____ in generating real-life violence.
    (a) no role
    (b) at least a limited role
    (c) a consistently moderate role
    (d) an undeniably major role
    (e) the most important role of all variables studied

15. Research in the United States has found that, compared to middle-class women, working-class women
    (a) are more critical toward television.
    (b) value TV more highly.
    (c) identify more strongly with characters and personalities.
    (d) all of the above
    (e) a and b

CRITICAL THINKING

1. Many consider the media to be primary agents of socialization. When we were growing up, many of our role models came from television. Think back to when you were growing up and the television role models that affected your life in some way. Do you think that these television icons influenced how you thought or acted? Yes or no? Can you think of specific examples? Who are your role models today?

2. Knight states that "ownership and control of the media are generally becoming more concentrated into a smaller number of larger corporate hands." What are the implications of this in terms of news coverage and program offerings?

3. Advertising plays a key role in all forms of media. We are constantly being bombarded by suggestions to use this, buy that, or go there. To what extent does advertising influence your decision to purchase a product or service? Will you buy a particular brand just because you like the ads? Is there a product or service that you won't use simply because of its ad campaign?

4. Box 5.2 deals with the issue of negativity in the news. The headline used here is from The Globe and Mail. How do you think this same story would have been handled by other news sources, such as your local newspapers? Do some news sources portray the news more negatively than others? Does this negativity verge on sensationalism?

TRUE OR FALSE?

T   F   **1.**   According to the chapter on religion, spirituality is currently on the upswing in North America.

T   F   **2.**   According to the chapter on religion, as a scientific discipline, sociology can judge the truth of religious claims.

T   F   **3.**   According to Durkheim, the idea of religion is inseparable from that of the Church.

T   F   **4.**   Durkheim felt that, religion would ultimately disappear.

T   F   **5.**   According to polls, more than half of Canadians currently attend church services weekly.

T   F   **6.**   The majority of Canadians who say they often think about questions pertaining to the origin and purpose of life, happiness, death, etc. exhibit religious commitment.

T   F   **7.**   According to the text, the drop-off in Catholic Church attendance in Quebec between 1965 and 1980 was due primarily to changes resulting from Vatican II.

T   F   **8.**   Canadian findings on the relationship between religious commitment and measures of social change, such as educational levels and workforce participation, provide moderate support for the secularization thesis.

T   F   **9.**   Research findings indicate that people who have formal religious affiliation are more anxious than those without formal religious affiliation.

T   F   **10.**   The fragment style of religion refers to the numerous religious options available within most of Canada's religious groups.

MULTIPLE CHOICE

1.   According to the text, all of the following early sociological theorists have strongly influenced the sociology of religion, except one. Who is the exception?
   (a)   Durkheim
   (b)   Parsons
   (c)   Marx
   (d)   Weber
   (e)   none (i.e., all of the above theorists were strongly influences)

2. When Marx called religion the "opium of the masses," he meant
   (a) once one becomes committed to religion, one cannot escape its clutches.
   (b) the satisfaction derived from religion is very intense.
   (c) the real effect of religion is due to the religious feeling itself, not the church or its organization.
   (d) religion soothes the exploited majority and prevents real economic solutions.
   (e) all of the above

3. In 1996, Pope John Paul announced that the theory of evolution
   (a) was the product of Satan.
   (b) should be ignored by faithful Christians.
   (c) was compatible with Christian faith.
   (d) was a scientific belief which had no real bearing on Christian faith.
   (e) was true.

4. According to Durkheim, the idea of a supernatural power is
   (a) an expression of humankind's inability to find answers to the ultimate purpose of life.
   (b) the result of teachings about miracles documented in the bible and elsewhere.
   (c) a symbol for collective sentiments.
   (d) all of the above
   (e) none of the above

5. In his book *The Protestant Ethic and Spirit of Capitalism*, Weber felt that the moral tone of capitalism could be traced to
   (a) ungodly material aspirations.
   (b) the edicts of the Roman Catholic Church.
   (c) the Protestant Reformation.
   (d) religious persecution of the Jews.
   (e) all of the above

6. According to Weber, the growth of monotheism is associated with
   (a) the spread of Judao-Christianity.
   (b) goals of political unification.
   (c) the decline of religion.
   (d) capitalism.
   (e) none of the above

7. Weber's concept of the "routinization" of religion refers to
   (a) the growth of sacred artifacts and rituals.
   (b) the social and political acceptance of a particular type of religion in a given society.
   (c) the process by which a personal following is transformed into a permanent congregation.
   (d) the growing boredom and perceived irrelevance of religion that occurs prior to a religious decline.

8. All of the following are dimensions of religion used by the Project Canada surveys to measure personal religiosity, except one. Which is the exception?
    (a) whether one has experienced God
    (b) one's belief in God
    (c) knowledge of the bible
    (d) frequency of praying
    (e) none (i.e., all of the above are dimensions)

9. According to the chapter on religion, the United Church of Canada's decision to ordain homosexual ministers illustrates
    (a) the coinciding of the pastoral and prophetic functions of the Church.
    (b) the dominance of the pastoral function of the Church over the prophetic function.
    (c) the dominance of the prophetic function of the Church over the pastoral function.
    (d) the lack of either a pastoral or prophetic function in the Church.

10. According to the text, the two major categories of religion in Canada by the year 2015, based on church attendance, are likely to be
    (a) evangelical Protestants and Roman Catholics.
    (b) evangelical Protestants and mainline Protestants.
    (c) mainline Protestants and Roman Catholics.
    (d) non-Christian religions and Roman Catholics.

11. Which of the following contradicts recent findings in regard to Canadian-American differences in religion?
    (a) There are proportionally more people who claim to be evangelical Protestants in the United States than in Canada.
    (b) There are proportionally fewer people who claim to be Roman Catholics in the United States than in Canada.
    (c) There is a higher proportion of commitment among Catholics and mainline Protestants in the United States than in Canada.
    (d) all of the above
    (e) none of the above

12. According to the text, having parents who regularly attended church is a _____ condition for religious involvement.
    (a) necessary
    (b) sufficient
    (c) a and b
    (d) none of the above

13. According to studies cited in the chapter on religion, those who are religiously committed in North American are more likely to be deprived
    (a) economically.
    (b) socially.
    (c) organismically (i.e., physically or mentally).
    (d) all of the above
    (e) none of the above

14. Compared to others, those who exhibit high levels of religious commitment are more likely to oppose
   (a) premarital sex.
   (b) homosexuality.
   (c) abortion when the child is unwanted.
   (d) all of the above
   (e) none of the above

15. Canadian studies of religious commitment indicate that, compared to their parents, teenagers are
   (a) much less religious.
   (b) somewhat less religious.
   (c) about equally religious.
   (d) somewhat more religious.
   (e) much more religious

CRITICAL THINKING

1. Marx worked from the assumption that religion is a human creation. Would it logically follow that it is a social creation? What are the social factors that define religion? What are some of the cultural aspects?

2. What variables are important to you in defining your own level of religiosity? Do you think that a universal measure can be created?

3. What are the implications of churches "competing" for members? How do you feel about the description of the British Columbia megachurch that is decorated to resemble a 1950s diner? Does it seem "right" that churches openly solicit membership?

4. How can the secularization thesis account for the decline in church attendance?

TRUE OR FALSE?

T   F   **1.**   According to the text, social stratification exists in all societies.

T   F   **2.**   The sociological concept of class has become widely used in the media.

T   F   **3.**   According to the chapter on social stratification, in sociological terms, socioeconomic status means the same thing as class.

T   F   **4.**   The Davis and Moore theory of stratification is a cultural product of the Great Depression in the United States.

T   F   **5.**   Viewing the major stratification theorists chronologically, it appears that the importance of class has steadily diminished.

T   F   **6.**   A recent Canadian study using 1986 Statistics Canada data found that those who received more education were more likely than others to come from families in which the father had a high level of education and a high-status occupation.

T   F   **7.**   According to Richardson's study, the concentration of ownership of large Canadian corporations is increasing.

T   F   **8.**   In 1995, the majority of female-headed, single-parent families were below the poverty line.

T   F   **9.**   The poverty rate among seniors has increased since 1980.

T   F   **10.**   Based on an absolute poverty criterion, Sarlo concluded that poverty in Canada has been virtually eliminated.

MULTIPLE CHOICE

1.   A low position in the social stratification system means that the individual
   (a)   is not employed.
   (b)   belongs to a racial minority group.
   (c)   has little power, prestige, and wealth.
   (d)   all of the above
   (e)   b and c

2. Achieved statuses play the largest role in societies that have _____ ranking systems.
   (a) closed
   (b) open
   (c) caste
   (d) aristocratic

3. Marx's writings on the Industrial Revolution were written about _____ years ago.
   (a) 350
   (b) 250
   (c) 150
   (d) 100
   (e) 50

4. Which of the following best describes Marx's prediction for capitalism, according to the chapter on social stratification?
   (a) the development of a social contract between the bourgeoisie and proletariat
   (b) increasingly severe strikes by the petite bourgeoisie
   (c) increasingly disorganized protest against working conditions
   (d) widespread protest ending in revolutionary upheaval
   (e) all of the above

5. According to Weber, all of the following are types of resources that underlying inequalities, except one. Which is the exception?
   (a) hereditary position
   (b) political power
   (c) prestige
   (d) wealth
   (e) none (i.e., he identified all of the above)

6. According to Davis and Moore, inequalities in society are
   (a) a functional necessity for society.
   (b) inevitable.
   (c) based on class distinctions.
   (d) all of the above
   (e) a and b

7. Which of the following criticisms have been aimed at the Davis and Moore theory of stratification?
   (a) Its major concepts are not measurable.
   (b) It does not explain gender differences in earnings.
   (c) It does not account for inherited wealth.
   (d) all of the above
   (e) b and c

8. All of the following theorists developed conflict approaches to stratification, except
   (a) Weber.
   (b) Davis and Moore.
   (c) Marx.
   (d) Lenski.
   (e) Dahrendorf.

9. Over the past century, all of the following occupational categories have decreased in relative size in the Canadian economy, except one. Which is the exception?
   (a) agricultural occupations
   (b) blue-collar occupations
   (c) service occupations
   (d) forestry/fishing/mining occupations
   (e) none of the above

10. Since the 1980s in Canada, the proportion of the labour force classed as
    (a) self-employed has increased.
    (b) unemployed has decreased.
    (c) working part-time or temporarily has decreased.
    (d) all of the above
    (e) none of the above

11. In the chapter on social stratification, a recent Canadian study using 1986 Statistics Canada data found that the most important factor affecting the status of an individual's current job was
    (a) that person's level of education.
    (b) that person's gender.
    (c) that person's race or ethnicity.
    (d) the status of that person's first job.
    (e) that person's intelligence.

12. In 1990, in which of the following occupations did the average earnings of women exceed that of men?
    (a) dentists
    (b) university teachers
    (c) bartenders
    (d) child care occupations
    (e) none of the above

13. All of the following describe Canadian patterns of income inequality over the past decade, except one. Which is the exception?
    (a) Real wages have stopped growing.
    (b) Income inequality has remained stable.
    (c) There are more unemployed.
    (d) Average family incomes dropped.
    (e) none (i.e., all of the above describe Canadian patterns)

14. The poverty line established by Statistics Canada
    (a) was about $10,000 per person in 1995.
    (b) occurs when the family spends more than 35 percent of their income on the basic necessities.
    (c) occurs when the family spends more than 55 percent of their income on the basic necessities.
    (d) is the level of income below which one is eligible for welfare payments in a given province.
    (e) none of the above

15. Approximately what proportion of Canadians can expect to be poor (i.e., below the low-income line) at some point in their working lives?
    (a) 1/10
    (b) 2/10
    (c) 1/4
    (d) 1/3
    (e) 1/2

CRITICAL THINKING

1. To what extent does your social class determine your life chances? Think about this in terms of education, employment, and religion.

2. Can a society exist without any levels of social stratification?

3. Box 7.2 points out the salary discrepancies between a factory worker's pay and that of an executive. How can we justify the gross differences in earnings? Is one job worth more? Is one more important than the other?

4. In Box 7.3, Christopher Sarlo reports on absolute and relative poverty. Are his definitions realistic? Are his measures reliable? Are they valid?

GENDER INEQUALITY: ECONOMIC AND POLITICAL ASPECTS

TRUE OR FALSE?

T   F   **1.**   Psychological studies confirm that, in general, the personality traits of men and women tend to be polarized.

T   F   **2.**   Sexual harassment occurs only when a system of dominance and exploitation exists.

T   F   **3.**   According to the text, the "working woman" is a recent phenomenon.

T   F   **4.**   The increase in female participation in the labour force is primarily a post-World War II phenomenon.

T   F   **5.**   In dual-earner families, wives rarely earn more than husbands.

T   F   **6.**   In Canadian government statistics, aboriginal peoples are not included in the category of "visible minority."

T   F   **7.**   Using Sheila Copps, Audrey McLaughlin, Alexa McDonough, and Kim Campbell as examples, Bashevkin argues that politics is one of the few "occupations" in which Canadian women are fairly represented.

T   F   **8.**   According to the chapter on gender inequality, anyone who is concerned about the subordinate position of women and seeks change is a feminist.

T   F   **9.**   There is no government policy in Canada aimed at gender inequality in politics.

T   F   **10.**   According to the text, employment equity programs have been criticized by most sociologists for "going too far," that is, for rapidly moving inexperienced women into jobs from which they were previously excluded.

MULTIPLE CHOICE

1.   The term "provider" describes the social role for Canadian men born in
   (a)   1925.
   (b)   1950.
   (c)   1975.
   (d)   all of the above
   (e)   a and b

2. If group A and group B are compared, and it is found that group A has a greater capacity to influence and control group B, it can be said that group A has more
   (a) authority.
   (b) power.
   (c) prestige.
   (d) all of the above
   (e) none of the above

3. According to the chapter on gender inequality, when measuring social inequality between groups, one must take into account the asymmetrical distribution of
   (a) power.
   (b) material well-being.
   (c) prestige.
   (d) all of the above
   (e) a and b

4. According to Chris Jackson, the value of work in the home, if done for market wages, would total _____ of the gross national product.
   (a) 1/3
   (b) 2/5
   (c) 1/2
   (d) 2/3
   (e) 3/4

5. A 1992 study found that women in Canada do _____ of all unpaid work.
   (a) 1/3
   (b) 2/5
   (c) 1/2
   (d) 2/3
   (e) 3/4

6. According to the chapter on gender inequality, the increase in the labour-force participation of Canadian women over the past few decades was caused by
   (a) an increase in the amount of leisure time which resulted from the mechanization of housework.
   (b) an increase in the demand for workers in service jobs.
   (c) higher levels of state support for the family.
   (d) all of the above

7. Women working full-time at paid work spend more time than men on
   (a) child care.
   (b) cooking.
   (c) maintenance and repairs.
   (d) all of the above
   (e) a and b

8. Husbands with full-time employed wives tend to reallocate their own time to the domestic chore(s) of
   (a) child care.
   (b) meal preparation and washing up.
   (c) house cleaning.
   (d) all of the above
   (e) none of the above

9. If women and men are concentrated in different occupations, the occupational structure is considered to be
   (a) sex-typed.
   (b) sex-segregated.
   (c) standard.
   (d) nonstandard.

10. In 1991, approximately what percent of the total Canadian labour force was female?
   (a) 35
   (b) 45
   (c) 50
   (d) 55
   (e) 60

11. Which of the following is excluded from the category of non-standard work?
   (a) self-employment
   (b) part-time work
   (c) limited-term contract employment
   (d) all of the above
   (e) none of the above

12. Currently, the average earned income of women is about _____ percent of the average earned income of men.
   (a) 45
   (b) 50
   (c) 55
   (d) 60
   (e) 65

13. The last group in Canada to be extended the right to vote by the federal government were
   (a) women in Quebec.
   (b) Inuit or registered Indians living on reserves.
   (c) people of Chinese, East Indian, or Japanese ancestry.
   (d) people documented to be mentally challenged.

14. According to Robinson, Saint-Jean, and Rioux, all of the following are new labels and stereotypes of female politicians, except one. Which is the exception?
    (a) one of the boys
    (b) "wife of ..."
    (c) feminist
    (d) champion
    (e) superwoman

15. Which of the following is an affirmative action measure to help ensure women's participation in politics?
    (a) setting quotas for women on riding nomination lists
    (b) documenting a party's commitment to gender parity
    (c) setting spending limits for nomination contests
    (d) all of the above
    (e) none of the above

CRITICAL THINKING

1. How are powerful female business executives commonly perceived? What about men who occupy "traditionally female" roles such as nurses, cashiers, or telephone operators? Are these perceptions changing quickly, slowly, or not at all? Why?

2. Are there biological differences that can explain the gender inequality, or is gender inequality due mainly to social and cultural factors? Be specific about the factors that account for gender inequality.

3. As present-day or future role models, what can your generation do to diminish inequalities of gender? Consider (a) how you can change your everyday behaviour, and (b) the kinds of public policy changes you would support.

4. What qualifications, resources, and support does a person need to run for Parliament? Are these qualifications, resources, and sources of support equally available for women and men? If you think there are male-female differences in this regard, what are the implications for the nature of Canadian democracy? Does the universal right of all citizens to run for office ensure that everyone can participate fully in politics?

RACE AND ETHNIC RELATIONS

TRUE OR FALSE?

T   F   **1.**   According to a popular social psychological explanation, anti-Semitism is the result of scapegoating when individuals are frustrated in their efforts to attain a desired goal.

T   F   **2.**   According to Marx, African slavery marked the beginning of the overthrow of capitalism.

T   F   **3.**   According to Marxists studying advanced capitalism, racist ideas are now used by employers to prevent the formation of class consciousness.

T   F   **4.**   Aboriginal peoples make up less than 5 percent of Canada's population.

T   F   **5.**   The intercolonial model for explaining inequalities between aboriginal people and others in Canada is a variant of conflict theory.

T   F   **6.**   During the 1992 Charlottetown Accord debates in which aboriginal self-government was proposed, many aboriginal women advocated voting against the Accord.

T   F   **7.**   Without new immigrants, Canada's population is expected to decline within 20 years.

T   F   **8.**   The majority of new immigrants to Canada still come from Europe.

T   F   **9.**   Canada accepts immigrants and refugees partly on humanitarian and compassionate grounds.

T   F   **10.**   In the 1950s, the immigration department regarded Italian immigration as desirable because Italian men were viewed as suited to low-wage, irregular, manual labour.

MULTIPLE CHOICE

1.   According to the text, the sociology of race and ethnicity is primarily about
    (a)   the origins, settlement, and life experiences of different ethnic and racial groups in Canada.
    (b)   the distribution of power and resources among ethnic and racial groups in Canada.
    (c)   self-concept and identity, including feelings of nationalism, among different ethnic and racial groups.
    (d)   all of the above
    (e)   none of the above

2. Which of the following was the most common typology for dividing humanity into races in the early part of the twentieth century?
   (a) black, white, red, yellow, and brown
   (b) Asiatic, African, and Indo-European
   (c) caucasian, negro, asiatic, and aboriginal
   (d) caucasoid, mongoloid, and negroid
   (e) occidental and oriental

3. Approximately what percentage of Canadians polled in 1990 agreed with the statement, "all races are created equal"?
   (a) 90
   (b) 75
   (c) 66
   (d) 50
   (e) 33

4. All of the following are examples of institutional racism, except one. Which is the exception?
   (a) Inuit were not allowed to vote until the 1960s.
   (b) Japanese and Chinese people were not allowed to work as pharmacists in British Columbia, even if they were born in Canada.
   (c) Carney Nerland, a member of the Aryan Nations, shot Leo LaChance, a Cree trapper, in cold blood, simply for being a native.
   (d) People in southern American states were required to pass difficult literacy tests to be eligible to vote, unless their parents had voted.
   (e) Nova Scotia historically had separate schools for blacks and whites.

5. Which of the following contradicts the primordialist explanation of prejudice?
   (a) Prejudice is a way of maintaining social boundaries.
   (b) Humans have a natural dislike for "nonfamily" members.
   (c) Ethnic and racial groups are like very large extended families.
   (d) The desire to be nepotistic is a conscious decision by individuals to favour their own.
   (e) none of the above

6. According to Marxists, racism serves to
   (a) justify the exploitation of groups of people.
   (b) support ideas that the owning class is socially superior.
   (c) confuse people about the way society really works.
   (d) all of the above
   (e) a and c

7. According to the chapter on race and ethnic relations, ethnic and racial labels are about
   (a) power.
   (b) politics.
   (c) material wealth.
   (d) political correctness.
   (e) language.

8. In which of the following areas are aboriginal people not much different from other Canadians?
    (a) life expectancy
    (b) rate of labour-force participation
    (c) housing conditions
    (d) infant mortality rate
    (e) none of the above

9. The main goal of the federal government's policy regarding aboriginal peoples in the first half of the twentieth century was basically
    (a) to bring Christianity to all aboriginal peoples.
    (b) to assimilate aboriginal peoples into mainstream Canadian society.
    (c) to eliminate poverty by providing training designed to help aboriginal peoples get jobs.
    (d) to segregate aboriginal peoples into reserves where their plight would become a marginal problem to mainstream Canada.
    (e) to allow aboriginal peoples to maintain parts of their own culture while simultaneously obtaining job skills required in modern Canada.

10. All of the following were features of residential schools for Indians in Canada, except one. Which is the exception?
    (a) The curriculum was primarily academic.
    (b) The residential schools were boarding schools.
    (c) Children were not allowed to speak in their native tongue.
    (d) Children were forbidden to speak to siblings of the opposite sex.
    (e) none (i.e., all of the above were features)

11. The central thesis of the internal colonial model of aboriginal development is that
    (a) aboriginal people failed to adequately adapt to changing social and economic conditions.
    (b) aboriginal lands were needed to allow settlement of people from France, England, and other European colonial powers.
    (c) aboriginal lands were confiscated as a result of conflicts between colonial powers in the United States and British North America.
    (d) aboriginal peoples were disempowered by governments.
    (e) none of the above

12. All of the following statements are true of the Quiet Revolution, except one. Which is the exception?
    (a) It occurred primarily during the 1950s.
    (b) It involved a questioning of the Catholic Church's authority.
    (c) The educational system became secularized.
    (d) The civil service in Quebec expanded.
    (e) none (i.e., all of the above are true)

13. What is the rank order of cities, from highest to lowest, by the proportion of immigrants in their total populations?
    (a) Montreal, Toronto, Vancouver
    (b) Montreal, Vancouver, Toronto
    (c) Toronto, Vancouver, Montreal
    (d) Toronto, Montreal, Vancouver
    (e) Vancouver, Toronto, Montreal

14. According to Fleras and Elliot, the sovereignty movement in Quebec receives the bulk of its support from
    (a) Francophone professionals who want to mobilize against foreign capitalist domination.
    (b) middle-class francophones looking to expand their opportunities in both the public and private sectors.
    (c) working-class Quebeckers railing against domination by non-Francophone owners.
    (d) a broad and diverse group of individuals interested in maintaining French language and culture.
    (e) a large segment of marginal and poor Quebeckers attracted to charismatic leadership and the appeal of a social movement.

15. Which of the following was the largest category of people who entered Canada in 1993?
    (a) refugees (all classes)
    (b) family-class immigrants
    (c) immigrant entrepreneurs
    (d) self-employed immigrants
    (e) assisted relatives of immigrants

CRITICAL THINKING

1. What do you think would have happened if the tables had been reversed and Leo LaChance, the Cree trapper, had "accidentally" shot and killed Carney Nerland, the self-proclaimed racist?

2. Table 9.2 outlines Canada's points system for the selection of independent immigrants. Do you think that the distribution of points is fair and equitable? Is this practice discriminatory? Why or why not?

3.   Think about Canada's multicultural policies. Do you agree with them? Do you think that immigrants should be expected to assimilate?

4.   Do you think that affirmative action is effective? Is it fair, or is it reverse discrimination?

INEQUALITY AMONG NATIONS: PERSPECTIVES ON DEVELOPMENT

TRUE OR FALSE?

T   F   **1.**   In the Philippine's export processing zone (EPZ), young women are hired by transnational corporations because of their cheap wages and docility.

T   F   **2.**   Most Canadians believe that poor countries are to blame for their own poverty.

T   F   **3.**   According to the chapter on inequality among nations, optimistic perspectives on economic development have greater merit than pessimistic ones.

T   F   **4.**   In order to compare the GDPs of different countries, national GDPs are converted into American dollars.

T   F   **5.**   Worldwide, more women than men are illiterate.

T   F   **6.**   The disparity between rich and poor people throughout the world is less than the disparity between rich and poor countries.

T   F   **7.**   According to the chapter on inequality among nations, Latin America was inhospitable to modern industry because its upper classes were already benefiting from precapitalist forms of exploitation.

T   F   **8.**   Peripheral economies differ from core economies in that they are more specialized than core economies.

T   F   **9.**   According to the chapter on inequality among nations, Japan's economic success resulted from sophisticated management techniques and the existence of a dedicated and disciplined work force.

T   F   **10.**   According to the chapter on inequality among nations, a strong national identity in Japan, South Korea, and Sweden has led to a strong desire in each country to develop as an independent economic force.

MULTIPLE CHOICE

1. Over the past fifty years, all of the following countries have made large moves up the rankings of economic development, except one. Which is the exception?
    (a) Japan
    (b) Singapore
    (c) Hong Kong
    (d) none (i.e., all of the above have made large moves)

2. The International Monetary Fund, the World Bank, and the G-7 are examples of
    (a) transnational corporations.
    (b) postindustrial organizations.
    (c) supranational agencies.
    (d) all of the above
    (e) none of the above

3. The gap between Third World and developed countries
    (a) narrowed in the 1960s.
    (b) narrowed in the 1970s.
    (c) narrowed in the 1980s.
    (d) narrowed in the first half of the 1990s.
    (e) has never narrowed.

4. Which of the following statements is false? Third World countries include millions of people who
    (a) are in a situation of near starvation.
    (b) have enough to eat.
    (c) are affluent.
    (d) are super-rich.
    (e) none (i.e., all of the above are true)

5. The number or figure representing the value of all goods and services produced in a country by its citizens in a year is referred to as
    (a) the gross national product.
    (b) the gross domestic product.
    (c) purchasing parity pricing.
    (d) the market value index.

6. Purchasing parity pricing
    (a) compares countries' incomes by what people can buy at home.
    (b) takes into account production-for-use values.
    (c) includes income earned in the underground economy.
    (d) all of the above

7. The country with the greatest disparity between rich and poor is
    (a) Brazil.
    (b) China.
    (c) the United States.
    (d) South Africa.
    (e) Russia.

8. In 1985, what proportion of Canada's economy was owned and controlled by foreign corporations, mostly a few giant transnationals?
   (a) 1/10
   (b) 1/4
   (c) 1/2
   (d) 2/3
   (e) 3/4

9. According to the chapter on inequality among nations, most of Canada's rich made it to the top through
   (a) inheritance.
   (b) hard work and education.
   (c) networking and "connections."
   (d) illegal activities.
   (e) a and b

10. According to Bairoch, the largest industrial powers in 1750 were
    (a) Britain and France.
    (b) Spain and Portugal.
    (c) China and India.
    (d) German and Sweden.

11. India's cotton industry was destroyed by
    (a) drought, famine, and epidemics.
    (b) an inability to produce high-quality cotton.
    (c) the slave trade.
    (d) unequal trade arrangements with England.

12. Which of the following Third World groups have benefited most from structural adjustment programs?
    (a) the poor
    (b) the middle classes
    (c) scientifically-trained professionals
    (d) elites

13. In which of the following countries did the pattern of development discredit modernization theory?
    (a) China
    (b) Japan
    (c) Mexico
    (d) Brazil
    (e) Russia

14. All of the following statements about dependency theory are true, except one. Which is the exception?
    (a) It was a response to the failure of other theories.
    (b) It was formulated in the 1940s and 1950s.
    (c) It initially focussed on Latin America.
    (d) It became influential in the United Nations during the 1960s and 1970s.
    (e) none (i.e., all of the above are true)

15. According to dependency theory, the major benefits to countries on the periphery are
   (a) jobs for local labour.
   (b) taxes and resource rents for the use of resources.
   (c) the transfer of skill and capital from core-based transnational corporations.
   (d) all of the above
   (e) none of the above

CRITICAL THINKING

1. Are you more inclined to support the "naively optimistic, Western-centric and mean-spirited approach" or the "deterministic, anti-imperialist and pessimistic approach" as an explanation for global inequality? What are the pros and cons of each perspective?

2. What are your thoughts on the ideas presented in Box 10.1? Do you think that the images of Third World nations as portrayed by the media are misleading? Were you surprised by Harris's accusation that these images are misleading?

3. Comment on the dependency theory, focussing specifically on Canada and the United States.

4. Can monetary assistance alone help to reduce the plight of Third World countries? Justify your position using evidence from the textbook and other sources.

TRUE OR FALSE?

T   F   **1.**   Our society is organized around the conventional nuclear family.

T   F   **2.**   Today's parents tend to rely heavily on relatives and friends to cope with parenting demands.

T   F   **3.**   According to the chapter on families, governments have increasingly recognized their responsibilities for the welfare of children through social assistance programs.

T   F   **4.**   Women are more likely than men to initiate separation and divorce.

T   F   **5.**   Studies indicate that children raised in the home have higher social development scores than children raised in good-quality day care facilities.

T   F   **6.**   "Baby blues" experienced by some women after delivery are a result of hormonal imbalances.

T   F   **7.**   Most adults who divorce do not remarry.

T   F   **8.**   The major problem facing lone-parent families is poverty.

T   F   **9.**   Because of government support of child care, less than half of Swedish mothers are involved in paid employment.

T   F   **10.**   Only a small minority of Canadian toddlers and infants are in day-care programs.

MULTIPLE CHOICE

1.   According to the text, which of the following statements concerning real families in the 1950s is false?
   (a)   People married earlier.
   (b)   There was less divorce.
   (c)   Realistic images of family life were televised.
   (d)   all of the above are false
   (e)   all of the above are true

2.   The family-values argument claims that
   (a)   understanding the culture of the family is the key to explaining its many social problems.
   (b)   there is only one legitimate model of the family.
   (c)   the values of the family have not become more diverse over time
   (d)   all of the above

3. According to the chapter on families, the family-values approach _____ the effect of social structure on behaviour.
   (a) ignores
   (b) exaggerates
   (c) minimizes
   (d) distorts

4. Cross-cultural studies indicate that in all cultures
   (a) the nuclear family is dominant.
   (b) the nuclear family provides care for the children.
   (c) the role of the father in conception is recognized.
   (d) all of the above
   (e) none of the above

5. All of the following are considerations when the family is viewed as a unit of social reproduction, except one. Which is the exception?
   (a) the provision of basic material needs
   (b) the nurturing of children
   (c) the socialization of children
   (d) the emotional support of adults
   (e) none (i.e., all of the above are considerations)

6. According to the chapter on families, "family" refers to
   (a) a legal union which outlines the rights and responsibilities of household members.
   (b) a social unit consisting of a man, a woman, and their unmarried children.
   (c) a biologically-determined descent system.
   (d) a set of social relationships that work to reproduce life.

7. In hunting and gathering societies, women typically
   (a) have children every year.
   (b) are forbidden extramarital sexual relations.
   (c) can choose infanticide if the child born is a burden.
   (d) all of the above
   (e) none of the above

8. In preindustrial Europe, individuals often
   (a) married at a young age and lived with the husband's parents.
   (b) married at a young age and lived with the wife's parents.
   (c) delayed marriage until land was available.
   (d) married late because of the sex-ratio imbalance.

9. The composition of households in preindustrial Europe was determined mainly by
   (a) labour needs.
   (b) family size.
   (c) family values.
   (d) religious background.

10. The fastest growing type of family in Canada today is
    (a) the single-parent family.
    (b) the cohabiting couple with or without children.
    (c) the traditional nuclear family.
    (d) the extended family.

11. Compared to heterosexual married or co-habiting couples, lasting relationships among gays and lesbians are _____ with regard to housework and child care.
    (a) more egalitarian
    (b) equally egalitarian
    (c) less egalitarian

12. Canadian and American studies indicate the most important reason for women prioritizing either family or paid work in their lives was
    (a) parental modelling of gender roles.
    (b) the degree of the women's success in the labour market.
    (c) adolescent peer influences, especially that of their best friends.
    (d) explicit and implicit messages of the wider culture.
    (e) none of the above

13. Approximately what percentage of marriages in Canada will end in divorce?
    (a) 30 percent
    (b) 40 percent
    (c) 50 percent
    (d) 60 percent
    (e) 70 percent

14. With the highly medicalized management of birth in our society, the typical experience of women after giving birth is unlikely to be
    (a) grief.
    (b) euphoria.
    (c) anger.
    (d) upset.
    (e) none of the above is unlikely

15. According to the text, which of the following is unusual after a divorce?
    (a) men voluntarily accepting and maintaining responsibility for the financial support of the children
    (b) women assuming custody of the children
    (c) eventually, men withdrawing from regular contact with the children
    (d) emotional turmoil for men
    (e) emotional turmoil for children

CRITICAL THINKING

1. Bonnie Fox states that "whereas women's concerns about family tend to focus on the difficulties of combining employment and child care, men's concerns probably centre on the growing elusiveness of the breadwinner role in this uncertain economy." Think about the traditional roles in a family. Would you be comfortable in a family environment where the roles were switched, for example, where the woman worked outside the home and the husband stayed home and cared for the children?

2. Fox concludes that our communities need to play an expanded role in supporting the family, particularly in Canada where "children are assumed to be a private responsibility." Do you think your community should be doing more to support families? If yes, what should be its expanded role? If no, give reasons for your position.

3. The turn of the nineteenth century brought about many changes in almost all social institutions. Along with social changes came a new conception of gender differences. How did the perceptions and realities of gender inequality change over time?

4. Furstenburg and Cherlin (1991) state that low income is especially significant because it reduces mothers' abilities to provide what researchers find to be most important for a child's adjustment after divorce – additional emotional support and a predictable daily schedule. How would the alleviation of financial problems alone solve this? Would more money be the panacea required to mend the disasters of divorce?

WORK AND OCCUPATIONS

TRUE OR FALSE?

T F   **1.**   The Industrial Revolution generally resulted in an increase in the skill level of individuals who produced goods.

T F   **2.**   Currently, the majority of Canadians are employed in the service sector of the economy.

T F   **3.**   In Canada today, over half of all jobs are nonstandard.

T F   **4.**   An American study of chief executive officers found that the majority reported working more than 60 hours per week.

T F   **5.**   Under "Fordism," the pace of work was controlled by owners who were directly involved in production.

T F   **6.**   According to the chapter on occupations, management can design computer-based jobs to either enhance or be detrimental to the quality of work.

T F   **7.**   The net effect of computer technology has been to create more jobs than are being replaced.

T F   **8.**   The most important determinant of job satisfaction among Canadians is the amount of money that they earn.

T F   **9.**   Older workers report more job satisfaction than younger workers.

T F   **10.**   Worker satisfaction tends to be higher in larger companies than in smaller companies.

MULTIPLE CHOICE

1.   The second industrial revolution involved all of the following, except one. Which is the exception?
    (a) the transformation of the feudal system of production
    (b) the development of mass-production technologies
    (c) an "administrative revolution" in office work
    (d) the rise of consolidated companies
    (e) none (i.e., all of the above were involved)

2. According to the chapter on work and occupations, the loss of jobs in the goods sector in Canada has been affected by
   (a) increased global competitiveness.
   (b) free trade agreements with the United States and Mexico.
   (c) lack of skilled Canadian workers.
   (d) all of the above
   (e) a and b

3. In terms of actual job shifts in the Canadian occupational structure, there has been
   (a) an increase in high-skill, knowledge-based work.
   (b) an increase in low-skill, low-paying service jobs.
   (c) both
   (d) neither

4. Which of the following sectors has the highest proportion of nonstandard work?
   (a) public administration
   (b) construction
   (c) manufacturing
   (d) retail trade
   (e) natural-resource-based

5. Current interest in shortening the work week is primarily motivated by
   (a) inefficiencies that result from "burnout."
   (b) increasing interest in and access to leisure pursuits.
   (c) an aging and tiring workforce.
   (d) the desire to create more employment.
   (e) the need to bolster the family.

6. According to early studies, all of the following are characteristics of a professional occupation, except one. Which is the exception?
   (a) Its members are highly paid and respected in public.
   (b) It controls a special body of abstract knowledge.
   (c) It is autonomous.
   (d) Workers have authority over clients.
   (e) none (i.e. all of the above are characteristics)

7. All of the following occupations are semiprofessions, except one. Which is the exception?
   (a) nursing
   (b) teaching
   (c) engineering
   (d) law
   (e) accounting

8. Which of the following statements contradicts Weber's views on bureaucracy?
    (a) Bureaucracies are the most efficient form for reaching the goals of capitalism.
    (b) Bureaucracies involve a complex division of labour.
    (c) Bureaucracies involve a clear hierarchy of authority.
    (d) In bureaucracies, routine situations are handled by client-oriented workers who have a wide latitude of discretion.
    (e) none (i.e., all of the above support Weber's views)

9. Time and motion studies are most directly associated with
    (a) Taylorism.
    (b) Fordism.
    (c) human relations management.
    (d) bureaucracy.
    (e) Japanese management techniques.

10. Workplace participation programs are typically employed by managers operating under the _____ model of work organization.
    (a) Taylorist or scientific management
    (b) Fordist
    (c) human relations
    (d) bureaucratic
    (e) Japanese

11. Research on Japanese production techniques used in automobile manufacturing indicates that the speed of the assembly line was determined by
    (a) managers.
    (b) workers.
    (c) the computerized assembly-line technology.
    (d) all of the above
    (e) a and c

12. All of the following are principles of Japanese production techniques, except one. Which is the exception?
    (a) Potential workers with pro-union attitudes are weeded out.
    (b) Attempts are made to have all workers exert the same amount of effort.
    (c) Workers are encouraged to help speed up their jobs.
    (d) none (i.e., all of the above are principles)

13. Currently, the "glass ceiling" for women in Canada begins at the level of
    (a) full-time workers.
    (b) managers.
    (c) senior managers.
    (d) chief executive officers.
    (e) all of the above

14. According to a study by the Foundation for Future Leadership, female managers did a better job than male managers in all of the following categories, except one. Which is the exception?
    (a) keeping productivity high
    (b) handling frustration
    (c) generating ideas
    (d) meeting deadlines
    (e) problem solving

15. In evaluating their job satisfaction, female workers tend to compare themselves to
    (a) other women.
    (b) other men.
    (c) other men and women.
    (d) close friends and relatives.
    (e) all of the above

CRITICAL THINKING

1. Welsh states that "most of us who find ourselves in jobs that we don't like or that force us to work like a robot would probably quit or quietly cope." Is this the case with you? What would cause you to stay with a job you didn't like?

2. Today, some employers are asking for "Canadian work experience" when interviewing or screening for potential candidates. Do you think that is prejudicial or discriminatory? Why or why not?

3. Due to the vast amounts of information produced by companies, management needed efficient systems to organize their offices. This led to the creation of a white-collar job sector and the growth of bureaucratic organizations. With all these changes came an increase in the division of labour. Now that advanced computer technology is so widely used, do you think that we still need the same large number of administrators? Why or why not?

4. Myles (1991) states that "the issue for the future is not whether we will have a service economy, but what kind of service economy" we will have. How does that make you feel in terms of getting a satisfactory, high-paying job when you graduate?

TRUE OR FALSE?

T F **1.** According to the chapter on education, in a given society at a given time, the experience of schooling is roughly the same for most individuals.

T F **2.** According to Bowles and Gintis, the high school curriculum for the less privileged emphasizes obedience and respect for authority.

T F **3.** According to Bowles and Gintis, students from more-privileged family backgrounds learn the "IQ ideology," while those from less-privileged backgrounds do not.

T F **4.** According to Randall Collins, educational credentials are employed in the job market because they are a good measure of the acquisition of job skills.

T F **5.** According to segmented labour market theory, in order to do better in the job market, women need to get more education.

T F **6.** According to Willis in his book *Learning to Labour*, working-class male adolescents do not buy into the "IQ ideology."

T F **7.** According to Canadian studies, the expansion of universities since World War II has done little to reduce the class bias of the student body.

T F **8.** According to the chapter on education, women's university enrolments have surpassed men's in Canada.

T F **9.** According to the chapter on education, the introduction of French immersion programs in Anglophone public schools in Canada has tended to reduce the advantages of relatively privileged students.

T F **10.** The "new math" which entered the curriculum during the 1960s is cited in the text as an example of a reform that failed.

MULTIPLE CHOICE

1. All of the following are major questions asked by sociologists about the educational system, except one. Which is the exception?
(a) Who succeeds in school and why?
(b) How have interest groups like parents and teachers affected education, and why?
(c) How are changes in education related to changes in the economy, and why?
(d) What knowledge is transmitted in schools, and why?
(e) none (i.e., all of the above are major questions)

2. Which of the following is an element of the formal curriculum of the school?
   (a) writing
   (b) history
   (c) work habits
   (d) all of the above
   (e) a and b

3. According to the structural-functionalist perspective, adult roles are based on
   (a) work habits and initiative.
   (b) ethnic, gender, and social class background.
   (c) marks in school.
   (d) all of the above
   (e) none of the above

4. According to Dreeben, the fact that students are treated alike as members of an age-graded classroom contributes especially to learning the norm of
   (a) achievement.
   (b) independence.
   (c) universalism.
   (d) specificity.

5. Structural-functionalist theorists call for remedial help to deal with disadvantages that students experience as a result of
   (a) race or ethnicity.
   (b) language.
   (c) social class.
   (d) all of the above
   (e) a and b

6. Statistics show that, compared to boys, girls
   (a) get higher grades in school.
   (b) drop out less frequently.
   (c) both
   (d) neither

7. According to status-attainment models, the best predictor of success at work is
   (a) success at school.
   (b) extensive participation in extracurricular activities in school.
   (c) the need for achievement.
   (d) social class and connections.
   (e) race and gender.

8. The Economic Council of Canada called for the reduction of spending on higher education
   (a) in the 1960s.
   (b) in the 1990s.
   (c) both
   (d) neither

9. The idea that education increases the productive capacity of workers is agreed upon by
   (a) human-capital theorists.
   (b) Bowles and Gintis.
   (c) Parsons.
   (d) all of the above
   (e) a and c

10. Which of the following are examples of "cultural capital" in Canadian society?
    (a) learning classical music
    (b) learning "standard English"
    (c) learning First Nations culture
    (d) all of the above
    (e) a and b

11. Which of the following theoretical perspectives is most concerned with the standpoint of sociological researchers as they study education?
    (a) Parsonian structural-functionalism
    (b) interpretive theory
    (c) Bowles and Gintis's version of conflict theory
    (d) Collins's credential theory
    (e) human capital theory

12. According to Linda MacNeil, how teachers think about their work is rooted primarily in
    (a) their own class and cultural backgrounds.
    (b) the needs of capitalist society.
    (c) their working conditions.
    (d) all of the above
    (e) none of the above

13. According to the chapter on education, attempts by schools in Canada since the 1970s to make the streaming process more subtle and invisible have been effective with
    (a) students.
    (b) the public.
    (c) postsecondary institutions.
    (d) all of the above
    (e) a and b

14. According to the chapter on education, which of the following statements are true of the elementary school curriculum?
    (a) It is based largely on language arts and mathematics.
    (b) It encourages a teacher-centred pedagogy.
    (c) There is a substantial vocational content in the curriculum.
    (d) all of the above
    (e) none of the above

15. According to a 1992 report by the Economic Council of Canada, better-educated people
  (a) have higher-paying jobs.
  (b) have more secure jobs.
  (c) have more satisfying jobs.
  (d) all the above
  (e) a and b

CRITICAL THINKING

1. Which of the major approaches to the sociology of education (structural-functionalist, conflict, or interpretative) corresponds most closely to your own experience? Do you think that your preference is based on your class of origin, sex, and/or ethnic/racial background? Discuss this issue with one of your classmates whose class of origin, sex, and ethnic/racial background differs from yours. Does your classmate share your theoretical preference? Why or why not?

2. Is it important to you that your textbooks reflect your own cultural background? Why or why not? To what degree does this textbook reflect minority cultural backgrounds? To what degree does it reflect the dominant culture? Give examples from the book to make your case. How, if at all, would you change the textbook to reflect what you consider to be the proper balance between majority and minority cultures?

3. Do you think global issues should feature more prominently in public school curricula? Explain why or why not. If you believe they should, then how should content be decided? Who should make decisions about content? How can local issues and needs be incorporated in a more global curriculum – or should they be?

4. How well do you think the Canadian educational system measures up to educational systems in other countries? Justify your opinion using evidence from the textbook and other sources. What do you think accounts for differences in the quality of education between Canada and other countries? In answering this question, make sure you compare Canada to countries where you think the educational system is superior and those in which you believe it is inferior.

TRUE OR FALSE?

T F **1.** By 1800, over one-third of the world's population lived in places with a population of over 5,000.

T F **2.** According to the chapter on urbanization, one of the most important reasons for the growth of cities in the industrial era was progress in medicine and health which lowered the mortality rate.

T F **3.** The Bank Act of 1871 was one of the major reasons for the concentration of the Canadian population into a few urban centres.

T F **4.** At the time of their development, houses in Don Mills, Canada's first planned suburb, were very expensive.

T F **5.** The majority of families displaced by urban renewal programs in the United States prior to 1963 were non-white.

T F **6.** There is no single way of life associated with the postmodern city.

T F **7.** The majority of gentrifiers are individuals fleeing from the suburbs.

T F **8.** Gentrified neighbourhoods are the fastest growing residential neighbourhoods in the United States.

T F **9.** Gated communities are a Californian invention.

T F **10.** Modular architecture is an attempt to combat the trend towards despatialization.

MULTIPLE CHOICE

1. According to the chapter on urbanization, ancient cities served primarily as
   (a) granaries.
   (b) government and administrative centres.
   (c) centres of religious worship.
   (d) centres of trade.
   (e) all of the above

2. According to the chapter on urbanization, all of the following are important elements in the development of preindustrial cities, except one. Which is the exception?
   (a) development of literacy
   (b) existence of a food surplus
   (c) technological innovations
   (d) peace-keeping arrangements

3. The primary factor which prevented ancient and medieval cities from larger growth was
   (a) disease and plagues.
   (b) an insufficient agricultural surplus in the society.
   (c) lack of suitable construction material for dense populations.
   (d) peoples' preference for a rural way of life.
   (e) environmental degradation.

4. The two largest cities in Canada are
   (a) Toronto and Vancouver.
   (b) Toronto and Montreal.
   (c) Montreal and Vancouver.
   (d) Toronto and Calgary.
   (e) Calgary and Montreal.

5. Members of the Chicago School of Sociology employed all of the following methods to gather information on urban problems, except one. Which is the exception?
   (a) ethnographic field research
   (b) analysis of biographies
   (c) systematic surveys
   (d) examination of court and agency records
   (e) none (i.e., all of the above were used)

6. Which of the following terms does not fit with the others?
   (a) gemeinschaft
   (b) rural area
   (c) social disorganization
   (d) traditional society
   (e) none (i.e., all of the above fit together)

7. According to Burgess's model, second-generation immigrants typically resided in
   (a) the central business district.
   (b) the zone of transition.
   (c) the zone of working-class homes.
   (d) the zone of better residences.
   (e) the commuter zone.

8. In Burgess's model, illegal commercial activities tended to occur in
   (a) the central business district.
   (b) the zone of transition.
   (c) the zone of working-class homes.
   (d) the zone of better residences.
   (e) the commuter zone.

9. According to the chapter on urbanization, all of the following elements are part of the corporate city, except one. Which is the exception?
    (a) high-rise apartment buildings
    (b) big-box stores
    (c) downtown office towers
    (d) suburban industrial parks
    (e) shopping centres or malls

10. Which of the following contradicts the description of Don Mills, Canada's first corporate suburb?
    (a) Most social action took place in the backyard.
    (b) The costs of services were born by the developer.
    (c) Availability of public transit was a key planning consideration.
    (d) It was located on the fringe of the city.
    (e) none (i.e., all of the above describe Don Mills)

11. All of the following groups are typically part of the urban-growth machine, except one. Which is the exception?
    (a) developers
    (b) professional sports teams
    (c) utilities
    (d) businesses
    (e) none (i.e., all of the above are part)

12. Which of the following types of cities exists in pure form?
    (a) the edge city
    (b) the theme-park city
    (c) the dual city
    (d) all of the above
    (e) none of the above

13. Edge cities are a cross between
    (a) central cities and suburbs.
    (b) city and country.
    (c) working-class and middle-class neighbourhoods.
    (d) all of the above
    (e) none of the above

14. Which of the following groups of women is least likely to be attracted to gentrified neighbourhoods?
    (a) seniors on a fixed income
    (b) young, single women
    (c) women with high academic credentials
    (d) women in dual-earner families
    (e) women in professional and technical occupations

15. Theme-park cities are a product of
   (a) too-rapid urbanization.
   (b) the symbolic economy.
   (c) "smoke-stack chasing."
   (d) all of the above
   (e) none of the above

CRITICAL THINKING

1. Hannigan states that "three elements of prime importance characterized preindustrial cities: the existence of a food surplus in fertile valleys, which permitted the specialization of labour zones of dense settlement; the achievement of literacy among scribes, priests, and other elite members of society, which allowed for the keeping of financial and other records; and technological innovations, notably metallurgy, agricultural irrigation, and the harnessing of wind and water power for sailing and grain milling." Which of these three phenomena do you think was the most important and influential in the move from preindustrial to industrialized societies? Why?

2. Berger (1960) refers to the "myth of suburbia," by which he means a standardized and stereotyped view of the suburbs as uniformly middle-class, homogenous, conformist, child-centred, female-dominated, and hotbeds of sociability. Do you think that his depiction is still accurate? Why or why not?

3. Logan and Molotch (1987) present their idea of an "urban-growth machine," a loosely-structured coalition of local economic and political interest groups with a commitment to sustained growth and development. Urban-growth machines can include "businesses, property owners, investors and developers, politicians and planners, the media, utilities, cultural institutions (museums, theatres), professional sports teams, labour unions, and even universities." Palen (1995) says that urban growth machines pursue a narrow band of interests, sacrificing the sentimental and symbolic value of places – which is associated with jobs, neighbourhood, home, town, and community – in favour of a strict emphasis on land use as an investment and commodity to be bought and sold. Primarily on whose behalf do you think these urban-growth machines are acting?

4. Box 14.2 depicts a rather grim view of city living with its depiction of "gated communities." Would you want to live in this type of environment? Why or why not? What are the advantages and disadvantages of residing in a gated city?

SOCIOLOGY AND THE ENVIRONMENT

TRUE OR FALSE?

T F **1.** One of the major pioneers and precursors of the modern interest in the environment in sociology was Émile Durkheim.

T F **2.** The Chicago School of urban sociology generally ignored the relationship between human activity and the natural environment.

T F **3.** Environmental sociology has focussed on the environment as a factor that may influence or be influenced by social behaviours. In other words, the environment can function as a dependent or independent variable.

T F **4.** According to the chapter on sociology and the environment, as a subdiscipline within sociology, environmental sociology today is fairly narrow in its theoretical foundations and research agenda.

T F **5.** The idea of sustainable development suggests that it is possible to have continued economic growth, but not at the expense of the environment.

T F **6.** Typically, it is easy to mobilize local support when people are faced with a clear environmental threat.

T F **7.** The Love Canal environmental crisis ended when the Hooker Chemical Company agreed to pay for the relocation of families living close to the canal.

T F **8.** Research shows that adherence to the alternative environmental paradigm precedes grass-roots mobilization.

T F **9.** According to the chapter on sociology and the environment, the best predictor of whether people are likely to perceive risk is the degree to which people trust the ability of expert institutions to assess danger.

T F **10.** According to the chapter on sociology and the environment, "maximalists" in the Love Canal case were typically those with strong attachments to their homes and with occupational links to the chemical industry.

MULTIPLE CHOICE

1. Interest in the environment dates back only about twenty-five years for
   (a) anthropology.
   (b) sociology.
   (c) geography.
   (d) all of the above
   (e) a and b

2. Which of the following environmental paradigms promotes the idea of steady social progress and increasing material comfort?
   (a) human-exceptionalism paradigm
   (b) social-constructionist paradigm
   (c) environmental paradigm
   (d) economic-prosperity paradigm

3. All of the following are elements of what Cotgrove labels the "dominant paradigm" in relation to the environment, except one. Which is the exception?
   (a) belief in economic growth
   (b) preference for large-scale, centralized society
   (c) belief in law and order
   (d) confidence in science and technology
   (e) none (i.e., all of the above are elements)

4. All of the following are elements of what Cotgrove labels the "alternative paradigm" in relation to the environment, except one. Which is the exception?
   (a) belief in the public interest being more important than market forces in the economy
   (b) emphasis on self-actualization rather than material values
   (c) preference for small-scale society
   (d) belief in authoritative structures in which experts are influential
   (e) none (i.e., all of the above are elements)

5. A major attempt to bridge the difference between the dominant and alternative environmental outlooks can be found in the idea of
   (a) human-exceptionalism.
   (b) sustainable development.
   (c) communitarianism.
   (d) none of the above

6. Which of the following hypotheses predicts that environmental concern will eventually diffuse throughout all groups, regardless of the country's economic conditions?
   (a) economic-contingency hypothesis
   (b) broadening-base hypothesis
   (c) environmental-diffusion hypothesis
   (d) globalization hypothesis

7. Higher levels of support for environmentalism are found among
   (a) those with higher levels of education.
   (b) urban residents.
   (c) supporters of political liberalism.
   (d) all of the above
   (e) none of the above

8. According to the chapter on sociology and the environment, the key factor accounting for participation in recycling programs is
   (a) easy availability of curbside pickup.
   (b) positive attitudes about the environment.
   (c) fear of future environmental disasters.
   (d) all of the above

9. Recently in Canada, environmentalists have been identified as members of
   (a) the bourgeoisie.
   (b) the cultural elite.
   (c) the new middle class.
   (d) the working class.

10. According to the chapter on sociology and the environment, successful framing has the following three components:
   (a) embryonic, mature, and degenerate.
   (b) primary, secondary, and tertiary.
   (c) crisis, confrontation, and resolution.
   (d) diagnostic, prognostic, and motivational.

11. "Success-oriented environmentalists" are
   (a) people whose chief goal is to stop pollution and other activities that damage the physical environment.
   (b) people who are interested in environmental issues only if they gain financial rewards and occupational prestige.
   (c) individuals whose main concern is to change the way others view the world.
   (d) all of the above

12. Deep ecologists emphasize that
   (a) humans, as superior beings, should have a more profound understanding of and appreciation for nature.
   (b) humans must study nature scientifically.
   (c) humans are only one species among many on earth and have no special rights or privileges.
   (d) anthropocentrism is necessary to prevent environmental catastrophe.

13. Many people who take a political-economy perspective blame the environmental crisis on
   (a) communism.
   (b) industrialism.
   (c) politicians.
   (d) none of the above

14. According to the chapter on sociology and the environment, the primary victims of pollution are
    (a) women and children.
    (b) people who work for chemical companies.
    (c) disadvantaged people.
    (d) the elderly.

15. The sequence through which most social problems pass has been referred to as
    (a) the "treadmill of production."
    (b) the "environmental-management stages."
    (c) the "issue-attention cycle."
    (d) the "social-construction sequence."

CRITICAL THINKING

1. The dominant paradigm and the alternative paradigm offers two distinctly different ideas about nature and the environment. To which paradigm do you most adhere? Does the dominant paradigm seem somewhat "harsh" to you? Is the alternative paradigm realistic?

2. Box 15.1 is a fascinating look into the dispute between industrialization or progress and the environment. How did you feel after reading this piece? How would proponents of both the dominant and alternative paradigms react to this article? In layman's terms, whose side are you on? Why?

3. According to Hannigan, "by the early 1970s, stimulated by increased societal attention to urban decay, pollution, overpopulation, resource shortages, and so on, a number of sociologists began at last to study environmental issues. In 1973, the Society for the Study of Social problems established an 'Environmental Problems Division.'…In 1983, *Sociological Inquiry* became the first English-language sociological journal to publish a complete special issue…on 'environmental sociology.'" Why do you think that it took so long for such an important topic to come to the forefront of such an inquisitive discipline?

4. Box 15.2 deals with the highly controversial and tragic Love Canal episode. If you are not currently "environmentally active," would it take something like the Love Canal incident to prompt you to become more aware of and involved in environmental issues?

TRUE OR FALSE?

T   F   **1.**   "The revenge of the cradles" was a call for French Canadians to maintain a high birth rate.

T   F   **2.**   Over the past century, net migration has accounted for about three-quarters of Canada's population growth.

T   F   **3.**   According to the chapter on population, trends in international and internal migration have tended to increase the relative size of Ontario and British Columbia, while reducing the relative size of the Atlantic provinces.

T   F   **4.**   The number of deaths in Canada is decreasing.

T   F   **5.**   According to Malthus, left unchecked, population growth would proceed in an arithmetic progression, whereas resources would grow geometrically.

T   F   **6.**   Generation X is another label for children of the baby boomers.

T   F   **7.**   According to Marx, the problem of food production would disappear under "socialism" or "communism."

T   F   **8.**   The population of less-developed countries is young and growing rapidly, while the population of more-developed countries is aging and growing much more slowly.

T   F   **9.**   Recent Canadian opinion surveys reveal that the majority of Canadians believe that immigration should be lowered, or at least not increased.

T   F   **10.**   The concentration of Canada's current population is geographically distributed quite similarly to the population of the native population prior to the arrival of Europeans.

MULTIPLE CHOICE

1.   The study of population size, distribution, and composition is called
   (a)   fertility.
   (b)   demography.
   (c)   ethnography.
   (d)   social statistics.
   (e)   geography.

2. According to the chapter on population, adaptations to the declining birth rate in Quebec have included all of the following, except one. Which is the exception?
   (a) Bill 101, the Quebec Charter of the French Language
   (b) the federal Official Languages Act
   (c) the federal policy on Multiculturalism
   (d) the recognition of a distinct role for Quebec in immigration selection
   (e) none (i.e., all of the above are adaptations)

3. If one were to analyze the impact of income and education on the number of births, one would be treating fertility as
   (a) a dependent variable.
   (b) an independent variable.
   (c) a dummy variable.
   (d) an intervening variable.
   (e) a background variable.

4. The "picture" of a population at a given time, including its size, distribution over space, and composition (age, sex, marital status, etc.) is called
   (a) a population census.
   (b) a demographic snapshot.
   (c) the population flow.
   (d) the population stock.

5. Malthus categorized the prevention of births through infanticide, abortion, and other means he viewed as unacceptable, as
   (a) positive checks on the population.
   (b) preventive checks on the population.
   (c) natural checks on the population.
   (d) moral restraints.
   (e) none of the above

6. The current Malthusian-Marxist debate on population in Canada essentially has been
   (a) decided in favour of Malthus.
   (b) decided in favour of Marx.
   (c) discontinued as other societal issues have taken precedence.
   (d) none of the above

7. In the human-ecology perspective, all of the following factors affect population dynamics, except one. Which is the exception?
   (a) organization
   (b) technology
   (c) environment
   (d) power
   (e) population

8. Stage 2 of the demographic transition is characterized by
   (a) declining mortality and declining fertility.
   (b) high but fluctuating mortality, and high fertility.
   (c) low mortality, and low but fluctuating fertility.
   (d) none of the above

9. The most important factor affecting the increase of life expectancy in Canada is
   (a) better nutrition for children and teens.
   (b) improved medical treatment of degenerative diseases.
   (c) improved medical treatment of infectious diseases.
   (d) declining infant mortality rates.
   (e) improved social services for the aged.

10. Which of the following refers to the "period" rate, or the average number of children that would be born to a women in her lifetime if she were to pass through all her childbearing years?
   (a) cohort fertility rate
   (b) age-specific fertility rate
   (c) total fertility rate
   (d) none of the above

11. The estimated annual cost of having three children aged 10, 12, and 17 is about
   (a) $20,000
   (b) $25,000
   (c) $30,000
   (d) $40,000

12. On average, compared to their native-born counterparts, foreign-born Canadians are characterized by
   (a) lower incomes.
   (b) higher unemployment.
   (c) greater labour-force participation.
   (d) all of the above
   (e) none of the above

13. According to the chapter on population, all of the following were refugee groups, except one. Which is the exception?
   (a) blacks
   (b) the United Empire Loyalists
   (c) Hutterites and Mennonites
   (d) Jews
   (e) none (i.e., they were all refugee groups)

14. Which of the following is currently the fastest growing province or territory in Canada?
   (a) British Columbia
   (b) Ontario
   (c) Nova Scotia
   (d) Quebec
   (e) the Northwest Territories

15. The peak year for the rate of world population growth occurred in
   (a) the 1990s.
   (b) the 1980s.
   (c) the 1970s.
   (d) the 1960s.
   (e) the 1950s.

CRITICAL THINKING

1. How are demography and sociology related?

2. Tuberculosis, plague, cancer, AIDS – how has disease affected not only the crude death rate but the crude birth rate as well? What are some of the social implications that these diseases have, and had, on the living populations?

3. Explain the demographic-transition theory. How does Malthus's theory of population relate to this model? Are you a believer in Malthusian theory? Why or why not?

4. Beaujot states that "although people live longer, their additional years of life are not necessarily spent in good health." Do you agree with this statement? What variables affect the health of a population? Is any one variable more important than another?

TRUE OR FALSE?

T   F   **1.**   Disembedding is the process whereby one alters one's perceptions of the nature of things by considering them from a different standpoint.

T   F   **2.**   According to the author of the chapter on globalization, globalization has occurred in part because people have lost confidence in humankind's ability to increasingly control nature and society.

T   F   **3.**   According to the chapter on globalization, the Soviet Union was the main enemy of the West during the Cold War, and Russia has emerged as an equally important focal point of Western anxieties today.

T   F   **4.**   Because of globalization and the growing need for a transnational policing agency, the power and credibility of the United Nations has been growing steadily and sharply over the past decade.

T   F   **5.**   According to Albrow, "performative citizenship" occurs when citizens work towards a new global state.

T   F   **6.**   According to the chapter on globalization, transnational political mobilization on global issues has already occurred.

T   F   **7.**   According to the text, globalization inevitably leads to social homogenization.

T   F   **8.**   "Post-Fordism" has resulted in the transfer of jobs from the West to the low-wage East.

T   F   **9.**   Time-space compression is the result of technological processes that allow instant communication, fast travel, and the recording and retrieval of past events.

T   F   **10.**   The author of the chapter on globalization takes the view that the new forms of life and social relationships in a globalized world make the idea of society obsolete and in need of replacement.

MULTIPLE CHOICE

1. According to the chapter on globalization, sociologists have traditionally equated societies with
   (a) the community.
   (b) the nation state.
   (c) urban areas.
   (d) the global.
   (e) the household.

2. The idea that there are rational principles of understanding humanity and nature that apply to all times and places is known as
   (a) globalism.
   (b) multiculturalism.
   (c) homogenization.
   (d) universalism.

3. According to the chapter on globalization, Chinese society has been characterized by
   (a) universalism.
   (b) capitalism.
   (c) imperialism.
   (d) all of the above
   (e) none of the above

4. According to the chapter on globalization, what event marked the arrival of capitalism as the unrivaled world economic system?
   (a) the Bolshevik Revolution of 1917
   (b) the Great Depression
   (c) World War II
   (d) the recent collapse of state socialism in Eastern Europe
   (e) the return of Hong Kong to China

5. According to the chapter on globalization, the term "modern"
   (a) refers to the current time period.
   (b) conveys a quality of living.
   (c) is used when the new, the technically advanced, and the rational replace traditional ways.
   (d) all of the above
   (e) none of the above

6. Which term was used to describe the efforts by the United States and other advanced countries to bring Third World countries into the capitalistic economic system?
   (a) modernization
   (b) assimilation
   (c) homogenization
   (d) relativization
   (e) acculturation

7. According to the chapter on globalization, all of the following are levels of analysis in the study of social life, except one. Which is the exception?
   (a) the global level
   (b) the nation-state level
   (c) the household level
   (d) the community level
   (e) the psychological level

8. According to the chapter on globalization, American influence over the Third World operates primarily through
   (a) the International Monetary Fund.
   (b) the World Bank.
   (c) the North Atlantic Treaty Organization.
   (d) all of the above
   (e) a and b

9. According to the chapter on globalization, which of the following countries is currently suffering from "imperial overstretch"?
   (a) the United States
   (b) Japan
   (c) Russia
   (d) China
   (e) all of the above

10. According to Martin Jaques, in which of the following areas has the process of globalization been slowest?
   (a) culture
   (b) politics
   (c) investment
   (d) economics
   (e) production

11. All of the following scholars recognized the international orientation and expansion of economic development, except one. Who is the exception?
   (a) Wallerstein
   (b) Marx
   (c) Adam Smith
   (d) Frank
   (e) none (i.e., they all recognized this)

12. According to the chapter on globalization, "McDonaldization" refers to
   (a) the spread of fast food to the Third World.
   (b) the "Americanization" of the world.
   (c) the standardization of activities that can be carried out anywhere.
   (d) all of the above
   (e) none of the above

13. In the chapter on globalization, all of the following are listed as a global city, except one. Which is the exception?
   (a) Tokyo
   (b) Los Angeles
   (c) New York
   (d) London
   (e) none (i.e., they are all listed as global cities)

14. According to the chapter on globalization, the global media have especially popularized
    (a) American superstars.
    (b) Anglophone superstars.
    (c) Asian superstars.
    (d) Canadian superstars.
    (e) all the above

15. In his novel *Generation X*, Douglas Coupland describes one of the major problems facing people who live in a globalized culture as
    (a) Mcliving.
    (b) generational drift.
    (c) security craving.
    (d) terminal wanderlust.
    (e) keeping up with the Pepsi generation.

CRITICAL THINKING

1. Albrow maintains that "the food we eat, the vehicles we drive, and the news we see on television can equally be found anywhere in the world." He furthers this by stating simply, "the global has become local." Explain what he means by this in terms of cultural, financial, and social institutions.

2. Albrow says that "globalization creates controversy among sociologists, as well as provoking public and political concern. Is it a process that can be stopped?" In your opinion, can globalization be stopped? More importantly, should it be stopped? Why or why not?

3. Box 17.1 describes the sheer infinity of global implications. How often do you stop to think about the global implications of a single, everyday action, such as having a cup of coffee? Identify an example of a seemingly common event that, in actuality, is global.

4. According to Giddens (1991), "the more tradition loses its hold, and the more daily life is reconstituted in terms of the dialectical interplay of the local and the global, the more individuals are forced to negotiate lifestyle choices among a diversity of options." Do you feel that this is a good thing or a bad thing? Why?

DEVIANCE AND CRIME

TRUE OR FALSE?

T   F   **1.**   According to the chapter on deviance and crime, deviance refers to variation from a norm even if it is socially insignificant in terms of the reaction of others.

T   F   **2.**   According to the chapter on deviance and crime, by appealing his conviction on a charge of mercy killing, Robert Latimer became a moral crusader.

T   F   **3.**   According to Marxist theory, the criminal law is a resource for the capitalist class, but not the working class.

T   F   **4.**   According to Sutherland, white-collar criminals are like street criminals because they share a culture that rewards rule-breaking.

T   F   **5.**   Sociologically speaking, stabbing with an ice-pick is an example of a "technique of neutralization."

T   F   **6.**   In Cloward and Ohlin's theory of delinquency, almost all lower-class youths who lack legitimate opportunities for success learn how to achieve success through criminal means.

T   F   **7.**   In Hagan, Simpson, and Gillis's control theory, boys are presumed to be freer to engage in delinquent acts than girls.

T   F   **8.**   According to Durkheim, rule-breaking by members of a society decreases that society's social solidarity.

T   F   **9.**   According to Lemert, in the final stage in the process of becoming a deviant, the self-fulfilling prophecy of the labelling process operates.

T   F   **10.**   According to the chapter on deviance and crime, crime rates of most Eastern European nations exceed those of the United States.

MULTIPLE CHOICE

1.   According to the chapter on deviance and crime, moral crusades have attempted to define deviance as
      (a)   behaviours considered harmful.
      (b)   behaviours of questionable harm.
      (c)   behaviours of limited harm.
      (d)   all of the above
      (e)   a and b

2. According to the chapter on deviance and crime, which of the following are central features of the process of defining deviance?
   (a) power relations and motivated individuals
   (b) power relations and political processes
   (c) motivated individuals and political processes
   (d) political processes and social processes
   (e) political processes and legal processes

3. According to Erickson, the criminalization of psychoactive drugs in Canada was a result of
   (a) hostile attitudes toward minority groups.
   (b) fears of the spread of habits picked up during World War I.
   (c) the development of the notion of "child-saving."
   (d) all of the above
   (e) none of the above

4. All of the following categories of people are included in Spritzer's category of "social dynamite," except one. Which is the exception?
   (a) radicals
   (b) "youthful, alienated, and politically volatile" lawbreakers
   (c) the unemployed
   (d) the aged
   (e) none (i.e., all of the above are included)

5. The lack of fit between cultural goals and social-structural opportunities was labelled _____ by Merton.
   (a) strain
   (b) social-structural stress
   (c) anomie
   (d) innovation
   (e) rebellion

6. According to Robert Merton, the poor are overrepresented among those arrested because
   (a) they have abandoned society's values.
   (b) they are evil or stupid.
   (c) the police pick on them.
   (d) they have fewer legitimate opportunities for success.
   (e) their rebellion is likely to be criminalized.

7. Which of the following theories focusses on how individuals influence one another?
   (a) differential-association theory
   (b) Merton's strain theory
   (c) both
   (d) neither

8. Which of the following contradicts Cohen's subcultural theory of deviance among lower-class youths?
   (a) Youth deviance is a collective response.
   (b) Youth deviance is often instrumental (i.e., profit-oriented).
   (c) Youth deviance is a reaction against middle-class values.
   (d) Fighting and destroying property are common.
   (e) none (i.e., all of the above support Cohen's theory)

9. Hirschi lists all of the following as bonds to society, except one. Which is the exception?
   (a) attachments to conventional others
   (b) commitment to conventional institutions
   (c) belief in conventional values
   (d) involvement in conventional activities
   (e) supervision by conventional authorities

10. Which of the following variables is the key to conformity, according to Gottfredson and Hirschi?
    (a) self-control
    (b) high self-esteem
    (c) proper early socialization
    (d) lack of deviant associations
    (e) access to legitimate opportunities

11. Lemert labels accidental, hidden, or occasional deviance as
    (a) primary deviance.
    (b) secondary deviance.
    (c) master deviance.
    (d) non-deviant deviance.
    (e) none of the above

12. Which of the following areas has the highest crime rates in Canada?
    (a) the Yukon and Northwest Territories
    (b) the Western provinces
    (c) Quebec
    (d) the Maritime provinces
    (e) Ontario

13. All of the following types of crime are increasing in Eastern Europe since the breakup of the Soviet bloc, except one. Which is the exception?
    (a) organized crime
    (b) common theft and robberies
    (c) complex, international criminal conspiracies
    (d) police corruption
    (e) none (i.e., all of the above are increasing)

14. All of the following are associated with the medicalization of crime and deviance, except one. Which is the exception?
    (a) decriminalization
    (b) decentralization
    (c) imprisonment
    (d) therapy
    (e) none (i.e., all of the above are associated)

15. The cost to keep a person in prison in Canada is about _____ per year.
    (a) $25,000
    (b) $35,000
    (c) $45,000
    (d) $55,000
    (e) $65,000

CRITICAL THINKING

1. Box 18.1 deals with the highly controversial topic of mercy killing. What was your reaction to this article? Where do you stand on this issue? Are you a supporter of Latimer? Will there ever be a right answer to the question of mercy killing? If so, what do you think it will be?

2. In Canada, crime rates have historically been lower in the eastern provinces, and highest in the Yukon and the Northwest Territories. What do you think accounts for this?

3. Hagan, Simpson, and Gillis (1987) argue that families exert greater control over girls than boys by socializing girls to avoid risks and by supervising them more closely. In contrast, boys are encouraged by their families to take risks and be independent. As a result, boys are freer to engage in delinquent acts than girls. Do you agree with this? Why or why not? Provide an example that helps to illustrate your opinion.

4. Gartner briefly touches on a relatively new aspect of deviance and social control. She states that "some [American] states now administer capital punishment through private contractors…Perhaps as much, or more policing is now done through private security as through public law enforcement in many countries, including Canada; and the number of people employed by private police agencies equals or exceeds those employed by public police agencies (Shearing, 1992)." What are your reactions to this? If private policing is indeed surpassing the numbers of employed in the public policing profession, can we assume that the two have the same levels of effectiveness? If private forces are increasing, why are we maintaining the same numbers in public forces?

TRUE OR FALSE?

T F   1. According to the chapter on social movements and politics, relative-deprivation theory is a form of the breakdown theory of social movements.

T F   2. Early leaders in the CCF in Saskatchewan were primarily socialists from outside the province.

T F   3. According to Marxist theory, the disorganization of the masses of workers leads to social movements.

T F   4. In power-balance theory, partisans of change refer to people who have an interest in, but are not directly involved in, forming or opposing social movements.

T F   5. The Regina Manifesto of the CCF called for state ownership of the means of production.

T F   6. In every Canadian federal election in which it has run candidates, the NDP has received less support from Canadian workers than the Liberal party.

T F   7. The new social movements described in the text tend to form separate political parties.

T F   8. According to the chapter on social movements and politics, women in general are better off in countries where the lower classes are more powerful.

T F   9. Fragmentation decreases as globalization increases.

T F   10. According to Brym in the chapter on social movements and politics, globalization helps to ensure that new social movements like the women's movement promote universalistic goals.

MULTIPLE CHOICE

1. According to Tilly and his associates, collective protest increased in Western Europe between 1830 and 1930 during periods of
    (a) rapid urbanization.
    (b) increasing crime.
    (c) both
    (d) neither

2. According to the chapter on social movements and politics, social movements are formed under circumstances that _____ social solidarity.
    (a) undermine
    (b) are the result of
    (c) create
    (d) all of the above
    (e) none of the above

3. According to the text, which of the following is the most important determinant of the power of a social movement?
    (a) its size
    (b) its level of organization
    (c) its access to scarce resources
    (d) its legitimacy
    (e) its homogeneity

4. According to the chapter on social movements and politics, revolution takes place when the power ratio
    (a) approaches infinity.
    (b) reduces to about zero.
    (c) approximates -1.
    (d) is less than 1.
    (e) none of the above

5. In the chapter on social movements and politics, all of the following reasons are cited for the failure of New Brunswickers to engage in political conflict against K.C. Irving, except one. Which is the exception?
    (a) They were poorly organized.
    (b) There were not enough people affected.
    (c) They lacked time and money.
    (d) none (i.e., all of the above were reasons)

6. Writing a newspaper story about a social movement's purpose and importance is an example of
    (a) frame bridging.
    (b) frame amplification.
    (c) frame extension.
    (d) frame transformation.

7. According to the text, all of the following were conditions of Prairie farmers which helped give rise to the formation of the farmers' social movement, except one. Which is the exception?
    (a) Farmers' bank credit was controlled by Eastern Canadian banks.
    (b) The marketing of grain was controlled by Eastern Canadian corporations.
    (c) The low value of the Canadian dollar relative to the American dollar made farm machinery very expensive.
    (d) Disgruntled farmers could easily see many others facing similar economic problems.
    (e) none (i.e., all of the above were conditions)

8. The CCF was created in the
   (a) 1910s.
   (b) 1920s.
   (c) 1930s.
   (d) 1940s.
   (e) 1950s.

9. For most of the twentieth century in Canada, the struggle for citizenship rights has focussed on
   (a) civil citizenship.
   (b) economic citizenship.
   (c) political citizenship.
   (d) gender citizenship.
   (e) universal citizenship.

10. According to the chapter on social movements and politics, which of the following groups of people is least likely to be attracted to the new social movements?
    (a) teachers
    (b) business persons
    (c) students
    (d) journalists
    (e) actors

11. Which of the following types of feminists advocates policies aimed at pay equity and the elimination of gender discrimination in the workplace?
    (a) socialist feminists
    (b) radical feminists
    (c) liberal feminists
    (d) conservative feminists
    (e) none of the above

12. The police and the military are part of a society's
    (a) legislature.
    (b) judiciary.
    (c) coercive apparatus.
    (d) executive branch.
    (e) all of the above

13. Which of the theories listed below assumes that the distribution of power does not change much over time?
    (a) pluralist theory
    (b) power balance theory
    (c) elite theory
    (d) a and b
    (e) a and c

14. Under what conditions have Canadian workers tended to vote for the NDP?
    (a) when there is an economic crisis
    (b) when they are unemployed
    (c) when scandals have affected other parties
    (d) all of the above
    (e) none of the above

15. Working-class voter support for democratic socialist parties is strong in
    (a) Canada.
    (b) the United States.
    (c) Sweden.
    (d) all of the above
    (e) none of the above

CRITICAL THINKING

1. In the introduction of this chapter, Brym recounts his first attempt at forming a collective with a cause. He admits defeat. Has a societal issue ever fuelled your emotions so passionately that you felt you had to strike up a force and fight for the cause. If so, think back to a personal example, that might resemble Brym's, and analyze its failures or successes.

2. What role do you think government plays in the day-to-day operations of post-secondary institutions? Are there hidden agendas? What about the allocation of research monies – do you think the distribution of these funds and the type of research carried out are politically connected?

3. In the 1960s, it was proposed that people rebel when many of them experience relative deprivation, or an intolerable gap between the social rewards they feel they deserve and the social rewards they expect to receive (Davies, 1969; Gurr, 1970). Brym states that "according to this school of thought, people are most likely to rebel when rising expectations brought on by rapid economic development and urban migration are met by a sudden decline in social rewards received due to economic recession or war." To what extent do you believe this modern form of breakdown theory? Do you think that this theory can explain the social movements of our current times?

4. Do you feel that Canada is a true democracy? Why or why not?

TRUE OR FALSE?

T   F   **1.**   A theory is a set of claims about what exists and the interconnections among existing phenomena.

T   F   **2.**   According to Durkheim, in order for "social facts" to become apparent, the activity must be considered in its social context.

T   F   **3.**   Durkheim's analysis would support the idea that modern societies require a certain amount of social consensus.

T   F   **4.**   According to the chapter on sociological theory, Merton's classification of functions does not contribute to sociological theory.

T   F   **5.**   According to Marx, an alienated person is one who suffers from the societal condition of normlessness.

T   F   **6.**   According to symbolic interactionists, stigma is a characteristic of an individual.

T   F   **7.**   A major critique of ethnomethodology is that the descriptions of particular constructions of meanings are not generalizable.

T   F   **8.**   According to the chapter on sociological theory, some middle-range theories work best when the analysis is restricted to a limited sector of society and the social forces internal to it.

T   F   **9.**   Research shows that as people contribute more resources to the household (e.g., income and job status), they do less of the less-valued household work.

T   F   **10.**   According to the chapter on sociological theory, nobody has succeeded in building an empirically adequate theory of society from a variety of middle-range theories.

MULTIPLE CHOICE

1.   If researchers find a theory that is not supported by the data, the legitimate responses include
    (a)   rejecting the theory.
    (b)   providing an account of why the theory did not work.
    (c)   acknowledging that more research is required.
    (d)   all of the above
    (e)   none of the above

2. Comte advocated a(n) _____ approach to the study of society.
   (a) philosophical
   (b) humanist
   (c) interdisciplinary
   (d) psychological
   (e) scientific

3. The study of sociology as we know it today stems back to
   (a) the early Middle Ages of England.
   (b) nineteenth-century Europe.
   (c) turn of the twentieth-century America.
   (d) Judao-Christian moral study.
   (e) all of the above

4. The theories that are based on faith in human perfectibility as espoused by Enlightenment thinkers were
   (a) functionalist theories.
   (b) order theories.
   (c) conflict theories.
   (d) all of the above
   (e) a and b

5. Which of the following theories calls for radical social change as the only solution to social inequality?
   (a) conflict theories
   (b) functionalist theories
   (c) order theories
   (d) all of the above
   (e) a and b

6. Durkheim referred to relative normlessness as
   (a) mechanical solidarity.
   (b) organic solidarity.
   (c) altruism.
   (d) anomie.
   (e) alienation.

7. According to Merton's adaptation of functionalism, when a university acts as a source of potential marriage partners, it is said to have
   (a) a structural function.
   (b) a dysfunction.
   (c) a manifest function.
   (d) a latent function.
   (e) any of the above

8. According to the chapter on sociological theory, Karl Marx's thinking was influenced by
   (a) the Enlightenment.
   (b) the French Revolution.
   (c) the conservative reaction to the French Revolution.
   (d) all of the above
   (e) none of the above

9. According to Marx, the basic contradiction of capitalism is
   (a) between morality and economics.
   (b) that political, legal, and other non-economic factors lag behind economic development.
   (c) that production is social, but appropriation is private.
   (d) that religion seems like the solution, but it is not.
   (e) none of the above

10. In Marxist terminology, all of the following factors are part of the superstructure of society, except one. Which is the exception?
    (a) economic factors
    (b) religious factors
    (c) political factors
    (d) legal factors
    (e) none (i.e., all of the above are factors)

11. Which of the following theories interprets power in a zero-sum manner?
    (a) neo-Marxism
    (b) modern conflict theory
    (c) modern functionalism
    (d) all of the above
    (e) none of the above

12. Verstehende sociology holds that
    (a) the meaning of an activity is important for understanding its effects.
    (b) the meaning of an activity is irrelevant to understanding its effects.
    (c) an action's meaning is inherent in the act itself.
    (d) an action's meaning has no effect on its consequences.
    (e) a and c

13. According to Weber
    (a) capitalism facilitated the rise of bureaucracy.
    (b) bureaucracy facilitated the rise of capitalism.
    (c) bureaucracy and capitalism emerged simultaneously.
    (d) bureaucracy and capitalism are ultimately irreconcilable.
    (e) c and d

14. All of the following statements about middle-range theories in sociology are true, except one. Which is the exception?
    (a) They should be formulated as tendency statements.
    (b) They make causal claims about specific social processes.
    (c) They recognize the complexity of the social world.
    (d) They employ multivariate research methods.
    (e) none (i.e., all of the above are true)

15. According to radical feminists, the root of male power lies in
    (a) the genes.
    (b) the society itself.
    (c) the economy.
    (d) the family.
    (e) women themselves.

CRITICAL THINKING

1. Which do you think contributed more to the advancement of society: the Industrial Revolution's influence on technology, or the age of Enlightenment's influence on ideology? Why?

2. Are functionalist and conflict theories as credible today as some of the newer emerging theories, such as ethnomethodology and radical-feminist theory? Why or why not?

3. Marx was very clear about the alienation of workers in the late nineteenth century. According to Menzies, "by alienated, [Marx] meant that people could not reach their full human potential. Their potential was denied by the control that others exercised over their work." Do you think that workers in today's society are alienated? Yes or no? If yes, which workers? How and why are they alienated?

4. Choose a sociological theory and defend its merit and worth as a tool to understanding other components of the discipline (e.g., the role of functionalism in research). Identify shortcomings of the theory and how you think it could be improved.

TRUE OR FALSE?

T   F   **1.**   The practice of science differs from religion and common sense in that it encourages criticism.

T   F   **2.**   Science is founded on facts derived from direct observation.

T   F   **3.**   A tautological truth is one that is not falsifiable.

T   F   **4.**   According to the chapter on research methods, because one can never fully "step into another's shoes," social science explanations are never fully acceptable.

T   F   **5.**   The fact that people blush is an example of the Hawthorne effect.

T   F   **6.**   Random-digit dialling excludes households with unlisted telephone numbers.

T   F   **7.**   Self-administered questionnaires work best with open-ended questions.

T   F   **8.**   According to the chapter on research methods, measuring people's attitudes is a good way to study their behaviour.

T   F   **9.**   A senior citizen who gives his age as ten years younger than his actual age is an example of the problem of social desirability in surveys.

T   F   **10.**   Sociologists are more likely than historians to use historical evidence to test theories of social change.

MULTIPLE CHOICE

1.   According to the chapter on research methods, the purpose of sociological investigation is
   (a)   knowledge.
   (b)   understanding.
   (c)   to better the human condition.
   (d)   all of the above
   (e)   a and b

2.   Which of the following sources of knowledge establishes permanent truths that everyone accepts?
   (a)   religious faith
   (b)   science
   (c)   common sense
   (d)   all of the above
   (e)   none of the above

3. According to the chapter on research methods, personal intuition plays an important role in
    (a) natural science.
    (b) medical science.
    (c) social science.
    (d) all of the above
    (e) none of the above

4. In the context of the scientific method, which of the following words does not fit?
    (a) reproducibility
    (b) full disclosure
    (c) replication
    (d) falsifiability
    (e) none (i.e., all of the above fit this context)

5. According to the chapter on research methods, which of the following is the most important difference between social science and natural science?
    (a) Social science uses soft data, and natural science uses hard data.
    (b) Social science studies meaningful action, and natural science does not.
    (c) Social science tends to use controlled experiments, and natural science does not.
    (d) Social science is subjective, and natural science is objective.
    (e) none of the above

6. "Causality" is another word for
    (a) association.
    (b) correlation.
    (c) relationship.
    (d) all of the above
    (e) none of the above

7. Which of the following is an example of spurious relationships?
    (a) number of cigarettes smoked and incidence of lung cancer
    (b) poverty level and incidence of premature births
    (c) the number of fire trucks at the scene of fires and the amount of damage caused by fires
    (d) all of the above
    (e) none of the above

8. The assignment of test subjects to experimental conditions on the basis of chance is referred to as
    (a) randomization.
    (b) random sampling.
    (c) establishing controls.
    (d) establishing a control group.

9. If a person's sex is said to affect his or her income, sex is
    (a) the dependent variable.
    (b) the independent variable.
    (c) the control variable.
    (d) the hypothesis.
    (e) the effect.

10. The term external validity refers to
    (a) the accuracy of measurement.
    (b) the consistency of measurement.
    (c) the generalizability to a larger population.
    (d) verification of the results by outside parties.

11. Which of the following techniques is often employed by social scientists to eliminate the problem of external validity associated with experiments?
    (a) the survey
    (b) participant observation
    (c) personal interviews
    (d) secondary analysis of data
    (e) the field experiment

12. A sampling frame refers to
    (a) the list from which the sample is selected.
    (b) the final list of individuals who will actually take part in the study.
    (c) the population to which the results will be generalized.
    (d) the list of individuals who will not take part in the study.

13. An ethnography contains the written results of
    (a) an experiment.
    (b) a survey.
    (c) participant observation.
    (d) environmental behaviour.
    (e) all of the above

14. The "member test of validity" is a method for reducing the problems in participant observation research associated with
    (a) the Hawthorne effect.
    (b) ethnocentrism.
    (c) ethics.
    (d) "creating meaning."
    (e) all of the above

15. Which of the following is the central characteristic of the best-fitting line in a regression analysis?
    (a) the point at which the line crosses the x-axis.
    (b) the point at which the line crosses the y-axis.
    (c) the slope.
    (d) the correlation.
    (e) b and c

CRITICAL THINKING

1. Consider controversial and sensitive subjects, such as abortion, euthanasia, and homosexuality. Can you research such highly-emotional topics without compromising your objectivity?

2. Comment on and explain the Hawthorne effect. Why was this such an important sociological study? What is its significance today?

3. Think about the differences between qualitative and quantitative research. Which do you think you would prefer to practice? Why? What are the pros and cons of each?

4. Think about the demands of validity, reliability, and representativeness. How do they affect our ability to generalize in social research? Is one more important than the other? If so, which one?

CHAPTER 1: Why Sociology?

True or False?

1.	T	6.	F
2.	F	7.	T
3.	T	8.	F
4.	F	9.	F
5.	T	10.	F

Multiple Choice

1.	b	6.	e	11.	d
2.	d	7.	a	12.	c
3.	e	8.	b	13.	c
4.	b	9.	c	14.	e
5.	c	10.	b	15.	a

CHAPTER 2: Socialization

True or False?

1.	F	6.	T
2.	F	7.	F
3.	F	8.	T
4.	T	9.	F
5.	F	10.	T

Multiple Choice

1.	a	6.	d	11.	a
2.	e	7.	a	12.	b
3.	d	8.	b	13.	c
4.	a	9.	e	14.	a
5.	d	10.	e	15.	c

CHAPTER 3: Culture and the Postmodern

True or False?

1.	T	6.	T
2.	F	7.	F
3.	T	8.	F
4.	F	9.	T
5.	F	10.	T

Multiple Choice

1.	b	6.	c	11.	b
2.	a	7.	e	12.	d
3.	b	8.	b	13.	e
4.	c	9.	b	14.	d
5.	c	10.	c	15.	b

CHAPTER 4: Sexuality

True or False?

1.	F	6.	T
2.	F	7.	F
3.	T	8.	T
4.	F	9.	T
5.	T	10.	F

Multiple Choice

1.	a	6.	a	11.	d
2.	b	7.	d	12.	e
3.	d	8.	d	13.	c
4.	e	9.	b	14.	a
5.	c	10.	a	15.	c

Chapter 5: The Mass Media

True or False?

1.	T	6.	F
2.	T	7.	T
3.	T	8.	T
4.	T	9.	T
5.	F	10.	T

Multiple Choice

1.	c	6.	b	11.	b
2.	d	7.	b	12.	e
3.	d	8.	e	13.	d
4.	c	9.	c	14.	b
5.	a	10.	e	15.	e

Chapter 6: Religion

True or False?

1.	T	6.	F
2.	F	7.	F
3.	T	8.	T
4.	F	9.	T
5.	F	10.	T

Multiple Choice

1.	b	6.	b	11.	e
2.	d	7.	c	12.	a
3.	c	8.	e	13.	e
4.	c	9.	c	14.	d
5.	c	10.	a	15.	c

Chapter 7: Social Stratification

True or False?

1.	T	6.	T
2.	F	7.	T
3.	F	8.	T
4.	F	9.	F
5.	F	10.	T

Multiple Choice

1.	c	6.	e	11.	d
2.	b	7.	e	12.	e
3.	c	8.	b	13.	b
4.	d	9.	c	14.	c
5.	a	10.	a	15.	d

Chapter 8: Gender Inequality: Economic and Political Aspects

True or False?

1.	F	6.	T
2.	F	7.	F
3.	F	8.	T
4.	T	9.	T
5.	F	10.	F

Multiple Choice

1.	a	6.	b	11.	e
2.	b	7.	d	12.	d
3.	d	8.	b	13.	b
4.	a	9.	b	14.	c
5.	d	10.	b	15.	a

Chapter 9: Race and Ethnic Relations

True or False?

1.	T	6.	T
2.	F	7.	T
3.	T	8.	F
4.	T	9.	T
5.	T	10.	T

Multiple Choice

1.	b	6.	e	11.	d
2.	d	7.	a	12.	a
3.	a	8.	c	13.	c
4.	c	9.	b	14.	d
5.	d	10.	a	15.	b

Chapter 10: Inequality among Nations: Perspectives on Development

True or False?

1.	T	6.	F
2.	T	7.	T
3.	F	8.	T
4.	T	9.	F
5.	T	10.	T

Multiple Choice

1.	a	6.	a	11.	d
2.	c	7.	a	12.	d
3.	b	8.	b	13.	b
4.	e	9.	a	14.	e
5.	b	10.	c	15.	a

Chapter 11: Families

True or False?

1.	T	6.	F
2.	F	7.	F
3.	F	8.	T
4.	T	9.	F
5.	F	10.	T

Multiple Choice

1.	c	6.	d	11.	a
2.	b	7.	c	12.	b
3.	a	8.	c	13.	a
4.	e	9.	a	14.	b
5.	e	10.	b	15.	a

Chapter 12: Work and Occupations

True or False?

1.	F	6.	T
2.	T	7.	F
3.	F	8.	F
4.	T	9.	T
5.	F	10.	F

Multiple Choice

1.	a	6.	a	11.	e
2.	e	7.	d	12.	b
3.	c	8.	d	13.	c
4.	d	9.	a	14.	b
5.	d	10.	c	15.	a

Chapter 13: Education

True or False?

1.	F	6.	T
2.	T	7.	T
3.	F	8.	T
4.	F	9.	F
5.	F	10.	T

Multiple Choice

1.	b	6.	c	11.	b
2.	e	7.	a	12.	c
3.	c	8.	d	13.	b
4.	c	9.	d	14.	a
5.	d	10.	e	15.	d

Chapter 14: Urbanization

True or False?

1.	F	6.	T
2.	F	7.	F
3.	T	8.	F
4.	F	9.	T
5.	T	10.	F

Multiple Choice

1.	c	6.	c	11.	e
2.	d	7.	c	12.	e
3.	b	8.	b	13.	a
4.	b	9.	b	14.	a
5.	c	10.	c	15.	b

Chapter 15: Sociology and the Environment

True or False?

1.	F	6.	F
2.	T	7.	F
3.	T	8.	F
4.	F	9.	T
5.	T	10.	F

Multiple Choice

1.	b	6.	b	11.	a
2.	a	7.	d	12.	c
3.	e	8.	a	13.	b
4.	d	9.	c	14.	c
5.	b	10.	d	15.	c

Chapter 16: Population

True or False?

1.	T	6.	F
2.	F	7.	T
3.	T	8.	T
4.	F	9.	T
5.	F	10.	T

Multiple Choice

1.	b	6.	d	11.	a
2.	e	7.	d	12.	c
3.	a	8.	a	13.	e
4.	d	9.	d	14.	e
5.	b	10.	c	15.	d

Chapter 17: Globalization

True or False?

1.	F	6.	T
2.	T	7.	F
3.	F	8.	F
4.	F	9.	T
5.	T	10.	F

Multiple Choice

1.	b	6.	a	11.	c
2.	d	7.	e	12.	c
3.	e	8.	e	13.	b
4.	d	9.	a	14.	a
5.	d	10.	b	15.	d

Chapter 18: Deviance and Crime

True or False?

1.	F	6.	F
2.	F	7.	T
3.	T	8.	F
4.	T	9.	T
5.	F	10.	F

Multiple Choice

1.	c	6.	d	11.	a
2.	b	7.	a	12.	a
3.	a	8.	b	13.	e
4.	d	9.	e	14.	c
5.	c	10.	a	15.	c

Chapter 19: Social Movements and Politics

True or False?

1.	T	6.	T
2.	F	7.	F
3.	F	8.	T
4.	F	9.	F
5.	F	10.	T

Multiple Choice

1.	d	6.	b	11.	c
2.	c	7.	c	12.	c
3.	a	8.	c	13.	e
4.	d	9.	b	14.	e
5.	b	10.	b	15.	c

Chapter 20: Sociological Theory

True or False?

1.	T	6.	F
2.	T	7.	T
3.	T	8.	T
4.	T	9.	T
5.	F	10.	T

Multiple Choice

1.	d	6.	d	11.	b
2.	e	7.	d	12.	a
3.	b	8.	d	13.	a
4.	c	9.	c	14.	e
5.	a	10.	a	15.	d

Chapter 21: Research Methods

True or False?

1.	T	6.	F
2.	F	7.	F
3.	T	8.	F
4.	F	9.	T
5.	T	10.	T

Multiple Choice

1.	d	6.	e	11.	e
2.	e	7.	c	12.	a
3.	d	8.	a	13.	c
4.	e	9.	b	14.	b
5.	b	10.	c	15.	e

The *New Society* Web Site provides you with a vast array of opportunities for exploring sociology on your own and developing a deeper understanding of the material covered in the textbook. The main features of the site are summarized below.

Interactive Exercises

These 21 online activities will challenge you to use and develop ideas in the textbook, and then take online quizzes to evaluate your understanding of the material. You can listen to Karl Marx, Max Weber, and Émile Durkheim explain their theories of social change and criticize those of their predecessors; investigate the structure of virtual communities; or learn about the secrets to rapid economic growth that have been discovered by South Korea and the other "Asian Tigers." (These exercises are listed on the following pages, and Table 1 shows their corresponding textbook chapter(s).)

Online Research Projects

Each of these 21 research projects corresponds to a chapter of *New Society*. These projects use online resources to help you explore and develop key ideas in the textbook. You will be asked to write short essays based on your reading, data analysis, and problem-solving. You can view and assess the structure of initiation rites, read and evaluate conflicting documents about the feminist debate on pornography, analyze data about environmental practices in Canada, and much more. (These projects are listed on the following pages, and Table 2 shows their corresponding textbook chapter(s).)

Current Events

This list of magazine and newspaper articles will inform you of important sociological issues in the news. The items are grouped by each *New Society* chapter. You will be asked to report on how key ideas in the textbook relate to real-world events and how real-world events illuminate sociological ideas.

Web Links

Hundreds of carefully selected links to other web sites are grouped by each textbook chapter. Just a few examples of what you'll find here include a timeline that illustrates the development of society and sociology, major works of sociological theory, recent Statistics Canada data, and information on how to write a sociology research paper.

Programs and Careers

If you are considering a major in sociology, you will find this section of the site particularly useful. Here you will find information on careers in sociology and links to all departments of sociology in North America.

Community Forum

This section contains general information about using the Web Site and a brief biography of Robert J. Brym, the textbook's author. Beginning in the fall of 1998, student and instructor questionnaires will be posted there. We welcome your feedback and suggestions.

INTERACTIVE EXERCISES on the Web Site

http://www.harcourtbrace-canada.com

1. Talking Heads (Marx, Weber, and Durkheim Explain their Views of Society)

2. From Snow White to Star Wars: Fairy Tales and Childhood Socialization

3. Some Effects of Computer Technology on Aboriginal Cultures

4. Violent Interaction and Social Structure: The Case of Wife Abuse

5. The Characteristics and Values of World Wide Web Users

6. The Protestant Ethic and the Spirit of Capitalism in Ontario and Quebec

7. Testing Common Beliefs About Poverty in Canada

8. The Limits of Employment and Pay Equity Laws and Programs

9. Race and IQ

10. What Makes the Four Tigers Roar? (The Secrets of Economic Growth in Asia)

11. The Father Vacuum

12. The Future of Work

13. An Elitist University System?

14. MUDs, MOOs, and Virtual Communities

15. Environmental Change and Acute Conflict

16. Population Growth

17. Globalization: Who Benefits?

18. What Is Violent Crime?

19. Strikes and the Decline of the Labour Movement

20. Functionalist and Conflict Theories of Inequality

21. Constructing and Reading Tables: The Effect of Education and Region on Income in Nova Scotia and British Columbia

Table 1: INTERACTIVE EXERCISES by Textbook Chapter
(C=Chapter; E=Exercise)

E \ C	1	2	3	4	5	6	7	8	9	10	11	12	13	14	15	16	17	18	19	20	21
1	X																			X	
2		X	X																		
3			X						X												
4				X							X										
5			X		X																
6						X														X	
7							X														
8								X													
9		X							X												
10										X											
11											X										
12												X									
13													X								
14		X	X											X							
15															X				X		
16																X					
17										X							X				
18																		X			
19																			X		
20							X													X	
21																					X

117

ONLINE RESEARCH PROJECTS on the Web Site

http://www.harcourtbrace-canada.com

1. The Popularity of Sociological Theories

2. The Structure of Initiation Rites

3. Whose Culture Is This?

4. Feminism and Pornography

5. Media Bias?

6. Satanism, Ritual Abuse, and Other Mind-Control Conspiracies

7. How the Pie Is Sliced: Measuring Income Inequality in Canada

8. Women in the 1997 Canadian Federal Election

9. Blacks in Canada and the USA

10. Social and Economic Costs of War and Militarism: The British Case

11. The Long-Term Effects of Divorce on Children

12. Do Computers Liberate or Oppress?

13. Educational Standards: A Crossnational Perspective

14. Megacity Toronto

15. Environmental Practice in Canada

16. Demography Challenge: World Food Quiz

17. Multinational Network Structures: The Case of OECD Trade

18. Does Prison Deter Criminals?

19. Between Nation and State

20. Face-to-Face Interaction: A Conversational Analysis

21. Conducting a Survey on Personal Networks: A Matter of Life and Death

Table 2: ONLINE RESEARCH PROJECTS by Textbook Chapter
(C=Chapter; E=Exercise)

E\C	1	2	3	4	5	6	7	8	9	10	11	12	13	14	15	16	17	18	19	20	21
1	X																			X	
2		X																			
3			X						X												
4				X				X													
5			X		X																
6			X			X												X			
7							X														
8								X											X		
9									X												
10										X									X		
11	X										X										
12							X					X									
13													X								
14														X							
15															X						
16																X					
17																	X				
18																		X			
19								X											X		
20		X																		X	
21																					X

Reader Reply Card

We are interested in your reaction to *Student Learning Guide to Accompany New Society, Second Edition,* prepared by Deborah Boutilier. You can help us to improve this book in future editions by completing this questionnaire.

1. What was your reason for using this book?

    ☐ university course ☐ college course ☐ continuing education course
    ☐ professional ☐ personal ☐ other _____
       development   interest _____

2. If you are a student, please identify your school and the course in which you used this book.

3. Which chapters or parts of this book did you use? Which did you omit?

4. What did you like best about this book? What did you like least?

5. Please identify any topics you think should be added to future editions.

6. Please add any comments or suggestions.

7. May we contact you for further information?

    Name: _____

    Address: _____

    Phone: _____

(fold here and tape shut)

Larry Gillevet
Director of Product Development
HARCOURT BRACE & COMPANY, CANADA
55 HORNER AVENUE
TORONTO, ONTARIO
M8Z 9Z9